Lecture Notes in Computer Science 15427

Founding Editors

Gerhard Goos
Juris Hartmanis

The series Lecture Notes in Computer Science (LNCS), including its subseries Lecture Notes in Artificial Intelligence (LNAI) and Lecture Notes in Bioinformatics (LNBI), has established itself as a medium for the publication of new developments in computer science and information technology research, teaching, and education.

LNCS enjoys close cooperation with the computer science R & D community, the series counts many renowned academics among its volume editors and paper authors, and collaborates with prestigious societies. Its mission is to serve this international community by providing an invaluable service, mainly focused on the publication of conference and workshop proceedings and postproceedings. LNCS commenced publication in 1973.

Shunli Zhang · Liang-Jie Zhang

Editors

Internet of Things – ICIOT 2024

9th International Conference
Held as Part of the Services Conference Federation, SCF 2024
Bangkok, Thailand, November 16–19, 2024
Proceedings

 Springer

Editors
Shunli Zhang
QingHai Institute of Technology
Xining, China

Liang-Jie Zhang 🔟
Shenzhen University
Shenzhen, China

ISSN 0302-9743 ISSN 1611-3349 (electronic)
Lecture Notes in Computer Science
ISBN 978-3-031-77002-9 ISBN 978-3-031-77003-6 (eBook)
https://doi.org/10.1007/978-3-031-77003-6

This Springer imprint is published by the registered company Springer Nature Switzerland AG
The registered company address is: Gewerbestrasse 11, 6330 Cham, Switzerland

If disposing of this product, please recycle the paper.

Preface

With the rapid advancements of mobile Internet, cloud computing and big data, device-centric traditional Internet of Things (IoT) is now moving into a new era which is termed Internet of Things Services (IOTS). In this era, sensors and other types of sensing devices, wired and wireless networks, platforms and tools, data processing/visualization/analysis and integration engines, and other components of traditional IoT are interconnected through innovative services to realize the value of connected things, people, and virtual Internet spaces. The way of building new IoT applications is changing. We indeed need creative thinking, long-term visions, and innovative methodologies to respond to such a change. The ICIOT 2024 conference was organized to promote research and application innovations around the world.

ICIOT 2024 was a member of Services Conference Federation (SCF). SCF 2024 had the following 10 collocated service-oriented sister conferences: 2024 International Conference on Web Services (ICWS 2024), 2024 International Conference on Cloud Computing (CLOUD 2024), 2024 International Conference on Services Computing (SCC 2024), 2024 International Conference on Big Data (BigData 2024), 2024 International Conference on AI and Multimodal Services (AIMS 2024), 2024 International Conference on Metaverse (Metaverse 2024), 2024 International Conference on Internet of Things (ICIOT 2024), 2024 International Conference on Cognitive Computing (ICCC 2024), 2024 International Conference on Edge Computing (EDGE 2024), and 2024 International Conference on Blockchain (ICBC 2024).

This volume presents the accepted papers for the 2024 International Conference on Internet of Things (ICIOT 2024), held in Bangkok, Thailand, during November 16–19, 2024. ICIOT 2024 received 16 submissions, and we accepted 9 papers for the proceedings. Each was single-blind reviewed and selected by at least three independent members of the ICIOT 2024 International Program Committee.

We are pleased to thank the authors whose submissions and participation made this conference possible. We also want to express our thanks to the Organizing Committee and Program Committee members, for their dedication in helping to organize the conference and reviewing the submissions. We look forward to your great contributions as a volunteer, author, and conference participant in the fast-growing worldwide services innovations community.

September 2024
Shunli Zhang
Liang-Jie Zhang

Organization

General Chair

George C. Polyzos   Athens University of Economics and Business, Greece

Program Chair

Shunli Zhang   Qinghai Institute of Technology, China

Services Conference Federation (SCF 2024)

General Chairs

Ali Arsanjani   Google Cloud, USA
Wu Chou   Essenlix Corporation, USA

Coordinating Program Chair

Liang-Jie Zhang   Shenzhen University, China

CFO and International Affairs Chair

Min Luo   Georgia Tech, USA

Operation Committee

Jing Zeng   China Gridcom Co., Ltd., China
Yishuang Ning   Tsinghua University, China
Sheng He   Tsinghua University, China
Zhuolin Mei   Jiujiang University, China

Steering Committee

Calton Pu (Co-chair)	Georgia Tech, USA
Liang-Jie Zhang (Co-chair)	Shenzhen University, China

ICIOT 2024 Program Committee

Abu Bakar Abd Rahman	Universiti Malaysia Sabah, Malaysia
Razan Abdulhammed	Northern Technical University, Iraq
Abdurazzag Aburas	University of KwaZulu-Natal, South Africa
Abhishek Bajpai	Rajkiya Engineering College, India
Georgios Bouloukakis	Télécom SudParis, France
Françoise Sailhan	IMT Atlantique, France
Na Yu	Samsung Research America, USA
Roselyn A. Maaño	Manuel S. Enverga University Foundation, Philippines
Piyush Sinha	Space Application Centre, India
Sayed Mazhar Ali Shah	Mehran University of Engineering & Technology SZAB Campus Khairpur Mir's, Pakistan

Conference Sponsor – Services Society

The Services Society (S2) is a non-profit professional organization that has been created to promote worldwide research and technical collaboration in services innovations among academia and industrial professionals. Its members are volunteers from industry and academia with common interests. S2 is registered in the USA as a "501(c) organization", which means that it is an American tax-exempt nonprofit organization. S2 collaborates with other professional organizations to sponsor or co-sponsor conferences and to promote an effective services curriculum in colleges and universities. S2 initiates and promotes a "Services University" program worldwide to bridge the gap between industrial needs and university instruction.

The Services Sector accounted for 79.5% of the GDP of the USA in 2016. The Services Society has formed 5 Special Interest Groups (SIGs) to support technology- and domain-specific professional activities.

- Special Interest Group on Services Computing (SIG-SC)
- Special Interest Group on Big Data (SIG-BD)
- Special Interest Group on Cloud Computing (SIG-CLOUD)
- Special Interest Group on Artificial Intelligence (SIG-AI)
- Special Interest Group on Metaverse (SIG-Metaverse)

About the Services Conference Federation (SCF)

As the founding member of the Services Conference Federation (SCF), the first **International Conference on Web Services (ICWS)** was held in June 2003 in Las Vegas, USA. Meanwhile, the First International Conference on Web Services - Europe 2003 (ICWS-Europe 2003) was held in Germany in October 2003. ICWS-Europe 2003 was an extended event of the 2003 International Conference on Web Services (ICWS 2003) in Europe. In 2004, ICWS-Europe was changed to the European Conference on Web Services (ECOWS), which was held at Erfurt, Germany. Sponsored by the Services Society and Springer, SCF 2018 and SCF 2019 were held successfully in Seattle and San Diego, USA. SCF 2020 and SCF 2021 were held successfully online and in Shenzhen, China. SCF 2022 and 2023 were held successfully in Hawaii, USA. To celebrate its 22nd birthday, SCF 2024 was held on November 16–19, 2024, in Bangkok, Thailand.

In the past 21 years, the ICWS community has expanded from Web engineering innovations to scientific research for the whole services industry. Service delivery platforms have been expanded to mobile platforms, Internet of Things, cloud computing, and edge computing. The services ecosystem has gradually been enabled, value added, and intelligence embedded through enabling technologies such as big data, artificial intelligence, and cognitive computing. In the coming years, all transactions with multiple parties involved will be transformed to blockchain.

Based on technology trends and best practices in the field, the Services Conference Federation (SCF) will continue serving as the conference umbrella's code name for all services-related conferences. SCF 2024 defined the future of New ABCDE (AI, Blockchain, Cloud, BigData & IOT) and entered the 5G for Services Era. The theme of ICWS 2024 was Web-based Services for Metaverse Era. We are very proud to announce that SCF 2024's 10 co-located theme topic conferences all centered around "services", with each focusing on exploring different themes (web-based services, cloud-based services, Big Data-based services, services innovation lifecycle, AI-driven ubiquitous services, blockchain-driven trust service ecosystems, industry-specific services and applications, and emerging service-oriented technologies).

– Bigger Platform: The 10 collocated conferences (SCF 2024) were sponsored by the Services Society, which is the world-leading not-for-profit organization (501 c(3)) dedicated to the service of more than 30,000 worldwide Services Computing researchers and practitioners. A bigger platform means bigger opportunities for all volunteers, authors, and participants. Meanwhile, Springer provided sponsorship to best paper awards and other professional activities. All the 10 conference proceedings of SCF 2024 were published by Springer and indexed in the ISI Conference Proceedings Citation Index (included in Web of Science), Engineering Index EI (Compendex and Inspec databases), DBLP, Google Scholar, IO-Port, MathSciNet, Scopus, and ZBlMath.
– Brighter Future: While celebrating the 2024 version of ICWS, SCF 2024 highlighted the International Conference on AI and Multimodal Services (AIMS 2024) to build

the fundamental infrastructure for enabling AIGC services ecosystems. It will also lead our community members to create their own brighter future.

– Better Model: SCF 2024 continued to leverage the invented Conference Blockchain Model (CBM) to innovate the organizing practices for all the 10 theme conferences. Senior researchers in the field are welcome to submit proposals to serve as CBM Ambassador for an individual conference to start better interactions during your leadership role in organizing future SCF conferences.

Contents

Design an AutoCar Kit for Project-Based Learning in Autonomous Vehicle Programming for University Students

Khuat Duc Anh, Bui Phi Hung, Pham Thi Thuc Trinh, Nguyen Quang Hiep,
Vu Tuan Linh, and Phan Duy Hung$^{(\boxtimes)}$ (iD)

FPT University, Hanoi, Vietnam
{anhkd3,hungpd2}@fe.edu.vn, {hungbphe160274,trinhptthe160790,
hiepnqhe160317,linhvthe176900}@fpt.edu.vn

Abstract. Self-driving cars are a dynamically growing industry, fundamental to transportation and robotics, providing a higher demand for AI specialists. Nevertheless, as occurs with so many things, the theoretical understanding of abstraction in textbooks and modern curriculum is not as easily implemented by students. While numerous third-party companies are available in the market that provide kits and real-life guides and practices for self-driving cars, these products are often only for individuals and have quite high prices, making it difficult to apply in the classroom model. To solve this problem, this paper introduces the low-cost Autocar toolkit that university students can use to learn autonomous vehicle programming, which includes basic computer vision algorithms. Learning materials are designed for project-based learning, the ability to practice in groups, and implementation principles that focus on applying the approaches and techniques in computer vision. This approach is intended to address some of the difficulties the institution faces in procuring educational facilities and remove the gap between theory and practice in autonomous vehicle-related education. The AutoCar kit is suitable for classroom practice with groups of 3 members. This paper describes the hardware kit, the software materials, and the exercises. The result is an educational technology tool that contributes to training programming engineers for self-driving cars.

Keywords: autonomous car · low cost · computer vision · project based-learning · educational technology tool

1 Introduction

The current trend in technological development focuses on the integration of artificial intelligence with various industries, where autonomous vehicles represent a significant advancement in transportation and robotics. Alongside the global progress in AI technology development, the demand for educational resources to enhance expertise in this field is also increasing [1].

S. Zhang and L.-J. Zhang (Eds.): SCF 2024 - ICIOT 2024, LNCS 15427, pp. 1–14, 2025.
https://doi.org/10.1007/978-3-031-77003-6_1

Worldwide, there have been studies to develop educational programs on artificial intelligence and learning support tools, particularly for robotics and autonomous vehicles at different educational levels. For instance, the study by Buxton et al. introduced an AI and IoT curriculum for grades 7–10, and Chiu et al. developed an AI program for secondary school students [2, 3]. These studies emphasize the application of robotic models in education. At higher levels, we must highlight NVIDIA's prominence, including its practical kit products and courses [4].

Besides educational programs, we can observe the development of robotics and autonomous vehicle competitions such as the FIRST Robotics Competition and the SAE AutoDrive Challenge [5, 6]. These competitions are designed for university and high school students under the guidance of instructors and teachers, emphasizing the value of practical learning experiences and project-based learning approaches in robotics education. After reviewing several AI programs in Vietnam, we found that these programs have provided essential to advanced knowledge of AI and are regularly updated [7]. However, the application of technology for education in teaching the skills necessary for self-driving car technology is still limited in virtual environments and computer simulations. Only a few students have the opportunity to experience and practice using actual vehicle models directly. Although there is potential for good educational outcomes, the cost of kits that university students can use to learn about AI and autonomous vehicles is relatively high, making their practical application in education face many difficulties [8, 9].

Our research proposes to combine a set of technology tools for education called AutoCar to support teaching. This toolkit aims to integrate theoretical learning with practical experience in autonomous vehicles. The research aims to equip students with the practical experience necessary for development in the fields of autonomous vehicles and AI.

Based on the set objectives and market research, we have combined a simple model that includes components to assemble the Auto Car model, installation instructions and a set of documents containing practical exercises that can be performed with this model, open-source code for setting up the car and solutions for the exercises. The exercises are designed for learners to acquire the knowledge and skills to implement computer vision problems such as lane detection and lane keeping by Canny algorithm, traffic signal detection, and vehicle detection by the real-time object detection system YOLO on the car model. The product is designed to be suitable for students studying computer vision. The device is small and low-cost, making it suitable for group activities in the classroom.

Details about the AutoCar Kit will be presented in three sections. Section 2 of this paper introduces the materials included in the product and the benefits and knowledge it provides students. Section 3 describes in detail the hardware used to create the car model, including its size and design. Section 4 provides information on how the car model interacts with the user's computer. Finally, the conclusions and future work of the education kit are discussed in Sect. 5.

2   KIT Document

The goal of the practice kit is for students to learn the techniques used in autonomous vehicles, understand the related theories, and apply them in practice. The theoretical part of the kit will cover fields related to AI and autonomous vehicles such as Computer Science or Automotive Engineering. The concepts of AI here focus on computer vision and deep learning. Through studying and completing practical exercises in addition to classroom knowledge, students will gain:

- A basic understanding of autonomous vehicles and practical applications
- A basic understanding of computer vision, deep learning and practical applications

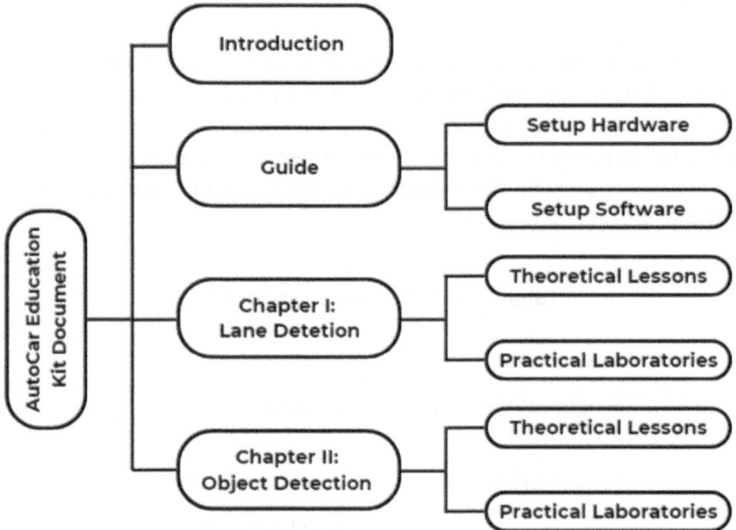

Fig. 1. Structure Diagram of the AutoCar Education Kit Document

The document's structure is divided into three main sections, each containing two exercises described in Fig. 1. The theoretical foundation of the content is designed based on the sequence of subjects in the FPT's current curriculum. The structure of the self-driving car program is available at some universities and in online courses, such as Udacity and Coursera [10, 11]. To support teaching, each document section includes essential theoretical content and practical exercises. Since a project-based method is applied in this course, the critical aspect of the kit will be the practical exercises aimed at designing and implementing a small-scale self-driving car suitable for running multiple units in a classroom setting.

The ultimate goal of the kit is for the car to follow the lane and recognize objects and signs on the map. The map will have 1 running lane, designed close to the actual scale and divided into 10 small pieces, like Fig. 2, to easily move and change shape.

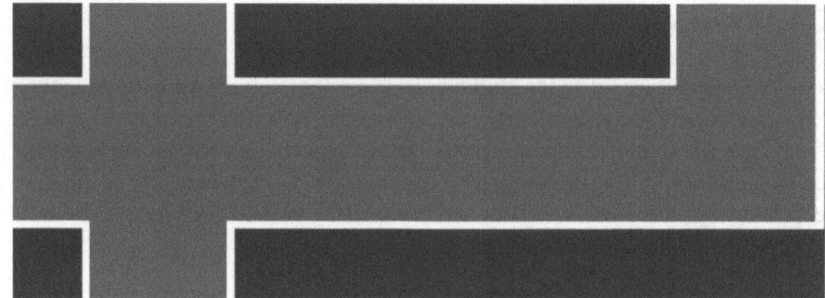

Fig. 2. The design of the map

2.1 Setup

This section's objective is to provide an overview of the car's hardware and software design. Additionally, it will guide students on how to assemble and install the necessary tools to enable the car to run and connect with a personal computer, thus preparing it for programming. Introducing students to the components' functions and the kit's operation is crucial to avoid any undesired incidents. The structure of the content in this section is detailed in Table 1.

Table 1. Installation Content Structure

Chapter	Section	Contents
Guide	Setup Hardware	Arduino Car Kit
		Camera
	Setup Software	Resource
		Python environment
		Pycharm/ Visual Studio Code
		Install Jupyter notebook
		Install necessary library
		Arduino IDE
		Transmit the code to the ACE kit
		Get the Camera's IP address

2.2 Lane Detection

2.2.1 Theory

Computer vision is a vast broad subject, and students in AI or autonomous vehicle fields usually have basic knowledge of image processing. This chapter focuses on applying techniques and algorithms to a practical problem: lane detection. The detailed content is described in Table 2. We will provide and explain in detail the relevant theoretical parts, including Calibration, the Canny algorithm, and perspective transformation techniques. All of these will be practiced in the lab at the end of the chapter.

Table 2. Contents of Chapter I

Chapter	Section	Contents
Chapter I: Lane Detection	Theory	Overview: Applying the edge detection Canny algorithm to operate the car in the lane
		Learning goals
		Related Knowledge
		Required background
		Problems: Calibration, Transform Perspective, Thresholding
	Laboratory	Guide
		Code

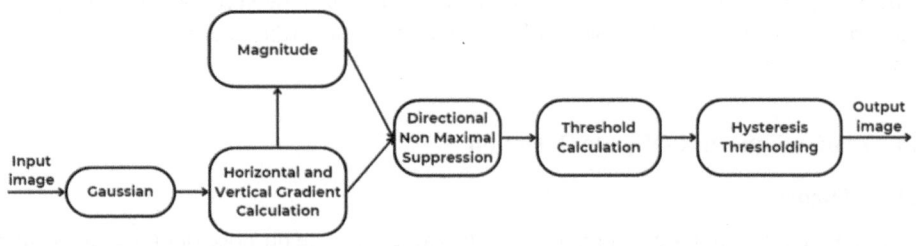

Fig. 3. Basic structure diagram of the Canny algorithm

Typically, the input image undergoes five steps in the basic Canny algorithm. Details of the sequence of steps are presented in Fig. 3.

2.2.2 Laboratory 1

The Laboratory will focus primarily on Canny – a straightforward algorithm for students that is widely taught in curricula and has abundant reference materials available. The Canny algorithm is one of the most efficient and widely used edge detection algorithms in image processing. Its effectiveness has been demonstrated in many papers in the past, achieving an accuracy rate of over 90% [12].

Upon completing this practical exercise, students will learn about real-time process-ing techniques and apply the Canny algorithm for lane detection. To effectively carry out these tasks, students need background knowledge in Python programming, the OpenCV library, and the Canny algorithm.

Fig. 4. Before and after calibration images

Fig. 5. Images before and after applying the transformation technique and Canny edge detection

Figures 4 and 5 depict the results after passing the input image through each pro-cessing step. It can be observed that extraneous scenes have been removed, leaving only the correct path visible. This serves best for making accurate decisions regarding the vehicle's movement.

2.3   Traffic Signs and Objects Detection

2.3.1   Theory

In this chapter, we include content on deep learning with the purpose of object and traffic sign recognition. Apart from providing students with foundational knowledge related to processing models, we also explain in detail the process of applying them to autonomous vehicles. The specific details of each section are described in Table 3.

Choosing a suitable model for processing is a relatively challenging task. Besides meeting basic requirements such as high accuracy and speed suitable for real-time pro-cessing, it also needs to be understandable and simple to fit university teaching programs. To meet these prerequisites while also adhering to hardware limitations, we decided to select the YOLO v5 model. This model has proven to be effective in real-world vehicle recognition tasks, with an accuracy exceeding 80% [13].

The network structure is illustrated in the diagram of YOLOv5 (default setup) in Fig. 6, comprising three main parts: (1) Backbone, (2) Neck, and (3) Head. After initial preprocessing, images undergo feature extraction in the Backbone, followed by feature

Table 3. Contents of Chapter II

Chapter	Section	Contents
Chapter II: Object Detection	Theory	Overview: Applying the YOLOv5 model to detect traffic lights and other vehicles
		Learning goals
		Related Knowledge
		Required background
		Problems: Data, YOLOv5 model
	Laboratory	Guide
		Code

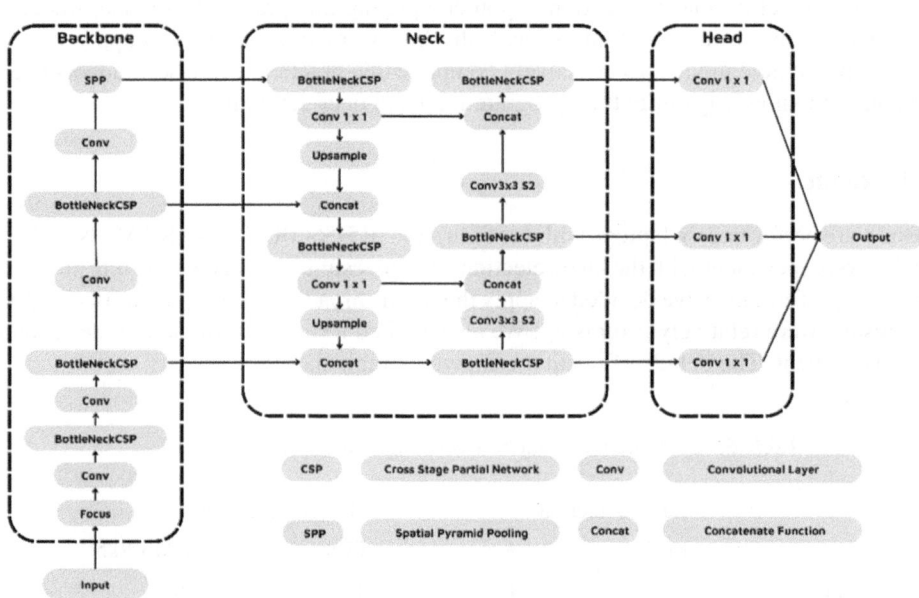

Fig. 6. Basic structure of the YOLO v5 model

fusion in the Neck. Subsequently, the Head network processes this information to produce a model and output detection results, including class, score, location, and size.

Although the pre-trained model already includes classes for traffic signs and vehicles, it does not fit well with our specific vehicle model. Therefore, we have decided to collect our own data to optimize the model's performance. Our dataset will consist of 1000 images captured from various angles using our kit, the details of which are described in Table 4.

Table 4. Dataset specifications

Class		Train	Test
Vehicle	Carkit	320	180
Traffic Sign	Straight	320	180
	Turn right	320	180
	Turn left	320	180
	Stop	320	180

2.3.2 Laboratory 2

With the knowledge provided, students will experience each step of applying the YOLOv5 model to object detection. Upon completing this practical exercise, students will understand basic programming with the YOLO model and how to apply it to a real-world vehicle model. To effectively complete this practical exercise, students need background knowledge in Python programming and deep learning.

2.4 Result

Tests were performed on laptops with configuration: R5-5500U - 16GB RAM - No GPU. In the first experiment with the lane detection lab, the results obtained were quite poor. To improve performance, we decided to apply the multi-threading technique. Subsequently, the results were relatively promising. We also applied a similar approach in the second lab experiment. The details of result are shown in Table 5.

Table 5. Compare the result between single-thread and multi-thread

	Lane Detection		Object Detection	
	FPS	Acc	FPS	mAP@0.5
Single-thread	1–3	42%	1–2	38%
Multi-thread	12–15	92%	10–12	86%

The User Datagram Protocol (UDP) is a communication protocol used in networking that operates on the transport layer of the Internet Protocol Suite. Unlike the Transmission Control Protocol (TCP), UDP is a connectionless protocol focusing on speed and efficiency. The switch from TCP/IP to UDP protocol resulted in a notable increase in frame rate from 8–9 fps to 13–15 fps. The details of the results are shown in Table 6.

Table 6. Compare the performance between TCP-IP and UDP

	Get image from ESP32	Transfer image
TCP-IP	7–8	3–5
UDP	22–25	22–25

3 Carkit - Hardware

Currently, Nvidia's Jet Racer kit is considered the best for autonomous vehicle practice [14]. However, its price exceeds $600 for a complete set, including the car chassis and Jetson Nano processor. There are cheaper options, such as the ELEGOO kit, which uses an ESP32 Camera combined with Arduino to control the motors and collect sensor data [15]. However, the size and hardware capabilities of the ELEGOO kit are not suitable for classroom environments and need to be more robust for complex artificial intelligence tasks in an autonomous vehicle model.

Therefore, we introduce the Autonomous Car Education Kit (ACE Kit), designed to support project-based learning and group collaboration for teams of 3 people. The kit includes a car model equipped with an ESP32S3-OV2640CAM, a motor control board L298, booster circuit XL6009, a car chassis FUT5024–1, two DC motors, two 18650 batteries, a battery box, USB-A to USB-C cable and an on/off switch. Additionally, the kit comes with detailed instructional materials (both printed and electronic) and a map of the car model.

To optimize costs and performance, we propose using personal laptops for artificial intelligence tasks instead of complex control boards within the kit. Hence, we choose the ESP32 Camera to capture images and transmit them to the laptop, which then sends control commands back to the DC motors. This approach ensures performance while minimizing the complexity of the circuit on the board.

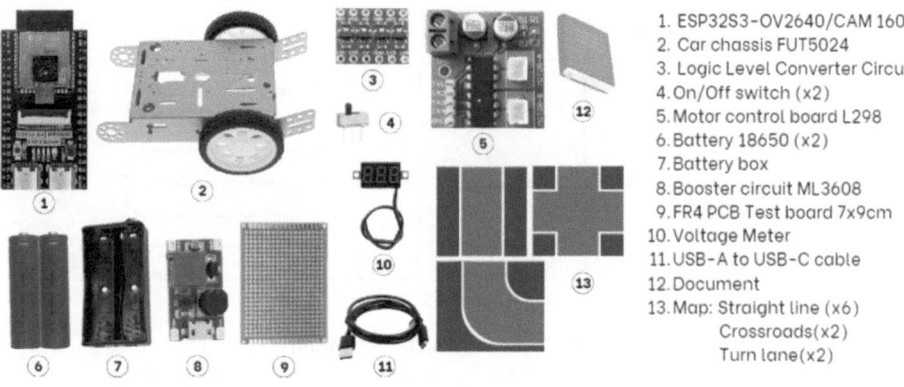

1. ESP32S3-OV2640/CAM 160°
2. Car chassis FUT5024
3. Logic Level Converter Circuit
4. On/Off switch (x2)
5. Motor control board L298
6. Battery 18650 (x2)
7. Battery box
8. Booster circuit ML3608
9. FR4 PCB Test board 7x9cm
10. Voltage Meter
11. USB-A to USB-C cable
12. Document
13. Map: Straight line (x6)
      Crossroads(x2)
      Turn lane(x2)

Fig. 7. Kit components of Autonomous Car Education kit (ACE-kit)

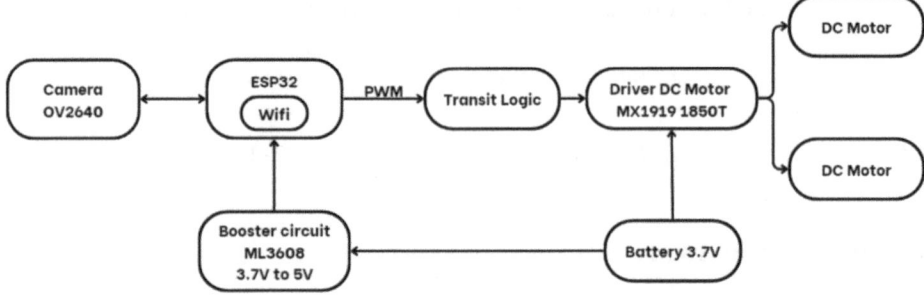

Fig. 8. Block diagram of Autonomous Car Education kit (ACE-kit)

The details about each component of the kit and the block diagram of the car are described in detail in Figs. 7, and 8. The use of two DC motors and a balancing wheel in the kit is intended to balance performance and cost, making vehicle control easier. The size of the car is reduced to 16×12 cm to suit classroom practice scales.

Our map will have 1 running lane, designed close to the actual scale and divided into 10 small pieces ($400 \times 400 \times 8$ mm) with intersections, straight segments, and curves, facilitating practical vehicle control exercises. The map pieces are connected using magnets and are made from lightweight and durable fomex material. Teachers and students can custom assemble them into different shapes, from simple to complex.

4 Carkit – Firmware

Intending to support the Computer Vision course, we have developed and provided code for controlling the autonomous vehicle using the selected hardware. This allows users to follow the instructions for setup without needing in-depth knowledge of IoT. The code is divided into three main parts: code for the ESP32-CAM, code for the motor control board, and code for the server to capture and share images among team members.

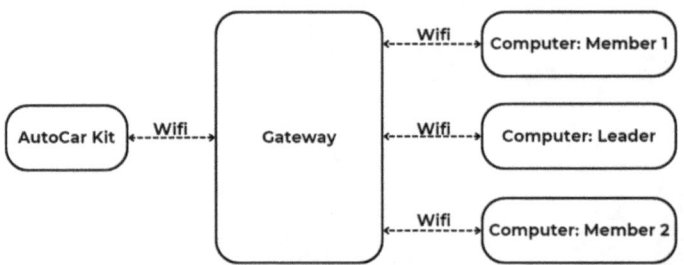

Fig. 9. Network structure diagram

Figure 9 describes the structure of the product's algorithm diagram. The vehicle and the user's personal computer will be communicated through a gateway.

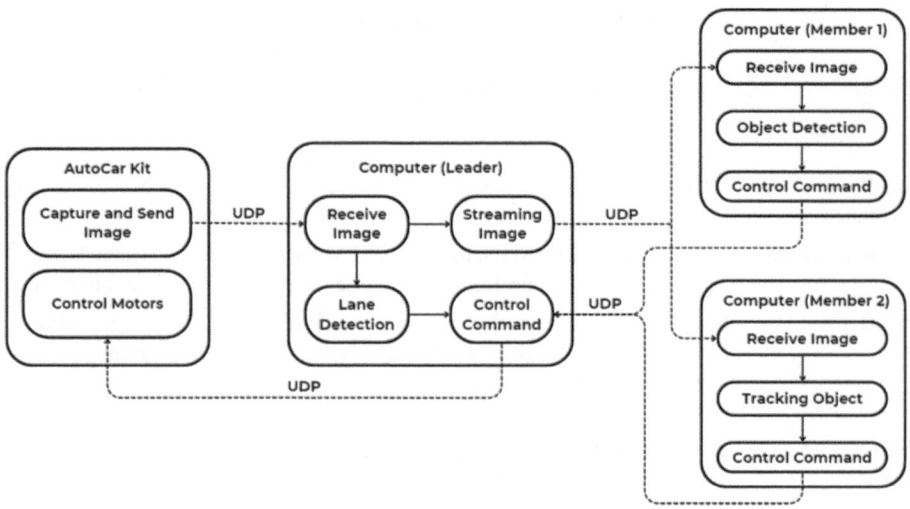

Fig. 10. Diagram of the signal transfer system

Data between the kit, Camera, and personal computer will be transferred according to the system in Fig. 10. The two main tasks designed for the kit are capturing and transmitting image data and controlling the motors to drive the car. These tasks run concurrently using FreeRTOS on the ESP32-CAM.

In Task 1, after the ESP32-CAM captures images from the camera, the input image signals are sent to the leader's computer via the UDP protocol. Here, the signals are divided into two tasks: streaming images to two member computers and lane recognition. The image streaming task transmits the image signals via UDP. After receiving the images from the leader's computer, the two-member computers process them for two different tasks. Once the three computers complete their respective image processing tasks, they produce control signal outputs. These outputs are sent back to the leader's computer via UDP, where they are compiled into a final control command and transmitted to the car.

The product stands out from existing solutions by optimally utilizing the capabilities of the ESP32 Cam. Since images need to be continuously transmitted and processed, task division and using the UDP protocol ensure greater stability and higher performance in image streaming. Therefore, even with the hardware design mentioned in this paper, the kit still meets the necessary tasks.

Table 7 compares our kit with several existing kits on the market. We have significantly reduced the cost by offloading AI processing tasks to personal computers and not integrating a Small AI computer into the model car. Additionally, the ability of personal computers to work together in processing different tasks is also a highlight of the AutoCar Education Kit.

Table 7. Compare the features of the kits

Criteria	JetRacer AI Kit	AI Machine Learning Starter Kit	ELEGOO Smart Robot Car	AutoCar Education Kit
Small AI computer	NVIDIA Jetson Nano	Raspberry Pi	No	No
Documentation	Manuals, tutorials	Manuals, sample projects	Manuals, code examples	Manuals, sample projects
Primary use	Professional racing competitions, AI research	AI education, personal projects	IoT education, automation	AI education, group projects
Included AI lessons	Deep learning, computer vision	Machine learning, neural networks	No	Deep learning, computer vision
Microcontroller	NVIDIA Jetson Nano	Raspberry Pi	Arduino	ESP32
Connectivity	Wi-Fi, Ethernet	Wi-Fi, Bluetooth	Wi-Fi	Wi-Fi
Price	~ 500$	~ 270$	~ 76$	~ 100$

5　Conclusion and Future Works

This paper presents a technology kit for education. It includes practical exercises on how to operate a lane-following vehicle that can detect traffic signals and objects, designed for college students using a project-based learning approach. This practical exercise integrates computer vision applications in autonomous vehicles. The AutoCar Kit includes an instruction manual, a map, a vehicle kit, and batteries. The manual includes hardware assembly, installation of AI application software on the vehicle model, detailed instructions on vehicle connection, and practice exercises. The documentation comprises two lab exercises covering the vehicle's two main functions in real-world scenarios, with steps that can be easily completed on any student's personal computer by closely following the instructions from setup to programming. Regarding the results achieved, initially, when using TCP/IP protocol, esp32 could only transmit 8–9 fps. After changing to UDP protocol and applying FreeRTOS, fps has improved to 13–15. Besides, this change also helps reduce an Arduino circuit. Thereby reducing vehicle size and reducing costs. We have also successfully tested dividing image processing tasks separately and performing them on three machines simultaneously.

For the next version, we aim to downsize the kit and add swarm operation capabilities and related practical exercises. We will reduce the size of the car to approximately 12 cm × 9 cm by designing the car frame ourselves. Consequently, The map size will also be reduced to 30 × 30 × 5 with a lane width of 16 cm. Thereby, it will improve convenience and flexibility during operation. Currently, our kit operates on a Wi-Fi connection for both receiving images from the camera and transmitting motor commands to the microcontroller. While this approach provides a response rate that meets the practical needs of experience for students, it can be hindered by Wi-Fi connection speeds. In the future, we aim to create a network for controlling multiple vehicles as a swarm so that they can work together on the same map without collision. When a class has multiple groups, with each group having one model car, we plan to add practice exercises that can combine the model cars. This will expand the scale of group practice with the kit and require coordination among more members. This paper is also a good reference for research directions of IoT [16, 17], Embedded Systems [18, 19].

References

1. Kozák, Š., Ružický, E., Štefanovič, J., Schindler, F.: Research and education for industry 4.0: present development. In: Cybernetics & Informatics (K&I), Lazy pod Makytou, Slovakia (2018)
2. Buxton, E., Javadi, E., Hagaman, M: Foundations of autonomous vehicles: a curriculum model for developing competencies in artificial intelligence and the internet of things for grades 7–10. In: Proceedings of the AAAI Conference on Artificial Intelligence, vol. 38, no. 21, pp. 23276–23284 (2024)
3. Chiu, T.K.F., Meng, H., Chai, C., King, I., Wong, S., Yam, Y.: Creation and evaluation of a pretertiary artificial Intelligence (AI) curriculum. IEEE Trans. Educ. **65**(1), 30–39 (2022)
4. Deep Learning Institute | NVIDIA. (n.d.). https://learn.nvidia.com/en-us/training/self-paced-courses
5. FIRST Robotics Competition. FIRST. https://www.firstinspires.org/robotics/frc. Accessed 23 May 2024
6. SAE AutoDrive Challenge. (n.d.). https://www.autodrivechallenge.com/
7. FPT Education Learning Materials. (n.d.). https://flm.fpt.edu.vn/gui/role/guest/CurriculumDetails?curid=21060
8. Bajracharya, B., Khan, M.S.: Prospects of autonomous vehicle learning kits in education systems. Inf. Syst. Educ. J. **21**(1), 32–38 (2023)
9. Bajracharya, B., Khan, M.S.: Autonomous vehicle education using learning kits. In: Proceedings of the EDSIG Conference, ISSN 2473, p. 4901 (2022)
10. Self Driving Car Engineer Nanodegree. https://www.udacity.com/course/self-driving-car-engineernanodegree--nd013. Accessed 31 July 2019
11. Welcome to the Self-Driving Cars Specialization. https://www.coursera.org/lecture/intro-selfdriving-cars/welcome-to-the-self-driving-cars-specialization-9l23h. Accessed 31 July 2019
12. Pavan, M.V.S., Ranjith, D., Reddy, K., Ismail, M.: Design and development of automated lane detection using improved canny edge detection method. Psychol. Educ. **57**(9), 1350–1358 (2020)
13. Kumar, S., et al.: Fusion of deep SoRt and YolOV5 for effective vehicle detection and tracking scheme in real-time traffic management sustainable system. Sustainability **15**(24), 16869 (2023). https://doi.org/10.3390/su152416869
14. JetRacer. (n.d.). NVIDIA Developer. https://developer.nvidia.com/embedded/community/jetson-projects/jetracer
15. ELEGOO Official. (n.d.). Smart Robot Car Kit v4.0 (with Camera). https://www.elegoo.com/products/elegoo-smart-robot-car-kit-v-4-0
16. Diep, V.T., Hung, P.D., Tung, T.D.: Energy saving solution for air conditioning systems. In: Dang, T., Küng, J., Takizawa, M., Bui, S. (eds.) FDSE 2019. LNCS, vol. 11814, pp. 618–628. Springer, Cham (2019). https://doi.org/10.1007/978-3-030-35653-8_40

17. Anh, K.D., Huynh, L.D., Hung, P.D.: A flexible internet of things architecture for data gathering and monitoring system. In: Dang, T.K., Küng, J., Takizawa, M., Chung, T.M. (eds.) FDSE 2020, pp. 189–199. Springer, Singapore (2020). https://doi.org/10.1007/978-981-33-4370-2_14

18. Linh, T.K., Hung, P.D.: Building a remote laboratory based on NVIDIA GeForce experience and moonlight streaming. In: Luo, Y. (eds.) CDVE 2021. LNCS, vol. 12983, pp 284–292. Springer, Cham (2021). https://doi.org/10.1007/978-3-030-88207-5_28

19. Hung, P.D., Duong, P.M., Giang, T.M., Diep, V.T.: Model-driven design for fast deployment of embedded systems. In: Proceedings of the 2nd International Conference of Intelligent Robotic and Control Engineering (IRCE), Singapore, pp. 138–142 (2019)

Research and Application of Distributed Energy Storage Monitoring System Based on Plug-and-Play Protocols

Jun Yang[✉], Mingfeng Shi, Xiaorong He, Yuke Zhao, Xin Lu, and Feifei Liu

China Gridcom Co., Ltd., Shenzhen 518109, China
gridcom@yeah.net

Abstract. The distributed energy storage system encompasses an extensive array of devices, communication protocols, and monitoring requirements. Owing to the multiplicity of these elements, attaining protocol adjustment and effective monitoring of the system has emerged as a pressing concern. To address the issue of energy storage protocol self-adaptation, a plug-and-play protocol mechanism has been formulated based on the Modbus protocol, which strengthens the protocol parsing and adaptation layer, thereby enhancing the overall efficiency of the system. In parallel, the communication network design of the distributed energy storage monitoring system has been implemented, and the upstream and downstream protocol processing flow has been described in detail. The distributed energy storage monitoring system, founded on the system architecture designed by this approach, has the ability to realize protocol conversion and self-adaptation, as well as to communicate with inverters of different brands and models. Finally, the photovoltaic (PV) energy storage system is presented as an exemplar of the energy storage monitoring program for both existing and new users. The energy storage monitoring module with the fusion terminal unit can unlock the energy storage and distribution network Internet of Things (IoT), thereby enabling comprehensive monitoring of energy storage, group regulation, and group control.

Keywords: Distributed Energy Storage System · Communication Protocol · Fusion Terminal Unit

1 Introduction

The accelerated advancement of smart grids and the growing proportion of green energy have led to a heightened focus on distributed energy storage systems, which play a pivotal role in the efficient utilisation of energy. However, the diversity of devices, communication protocols and monitoring requirements inherent to distributed energy storage systems (DESS) has given rise to the urgent need to develop solutions that facilitate the self-adaptation of system protocols and efficient monitoring. Accordingly, the objective of this study is to put forward a distributed energy storage monitoring method that enables protocol adaptation and energy storage monitoring via a plug-and-play mechanism [1, 2].

© The Author(s), under exclusive license to Springer Nature Switzerland AG 2025
S. Zhang and L.-J. Zhang (Eds.): SCF 2024 - ICIOT 2024, LNCS 15427, pp. 15–24, 2025.
https://doi.org/10.1007/978-3-031-77003-6_2

The plug-and-play mechanism enables the distributed energy storage monitoring system to access and manage different brands and models of energy storage devices via the conversion of multiple communication protocols. By introducing the plug-and-play protocol to achieve the rapid access of energy storage devices, the system maintenance cost can be reduced and the system operation efficiency can be improved. At the same time, the distributed energy storage monitoring method founded on the plug-and-play protocol can likewise realize remote monitoring and fault diagnosis of the energy storage equipment, and boost the stability and safety of the system [3]. The stability and safety of the system can be heightened [4]. Consequently, the distributed energy storage system monitoring based on plug-and-play protocol has important application prospects and popularization value.

2 Plug-and-Play Mechanism

The Modbus protocol is a prevalently employed communication protocol for energy storage systems in the industrial domain. Its fundamental principle is to achieve data and information exchange and control via serial communication between master and slave devices. Therefore, when constructing an adaptive energy storage monitoring system, it is requisite to conduct an in-depth analysis of the Modbus protocol and construct the adaptation layer in accordance with the actual application scenario [5]. The adaptation layer is constructed in accordance with the actual application scenario.

In the aspect of protocol parsing, the structure and format of Modbus protocol messages are analyzed by employing regular expressions and other techniques for matching and filtering the message content. This enables the extraction of key information, such as the device address, error code, and function code. This information is then utilized to parse the data related to the device type and power data, as shown in Table 1. The actual application process, namely the Modbus downstream group framing process, is accomplished by the utilization of the Modbus protocol's master address and function code, which are employed to facilitate the recognition of different PV inverter protocols on site and enable communication with inverters of various brands and models.

The following Table 1 gives a modbus protocol format definition and data type definition.

Through the adaptation to different device types and different communication interfaces in the construction of the adaptation layer, the access and monitoring of a variety of Modbus devices are achieved [6]. At the same time, we have also introduced dynamic configuration technology, allowing users to carry out real-time reconfiguration and context-aware configuration of the adaptation layer flexibly in accordance with actual needs.

The actual application process is primarily centered around the processing of Modbus uplink frames. The meticulous processing of Modbus uplink unframing encompasses two crucial steps: the meticulous frame checking and the precise unframing. Once the unframing process is completed, the Modbus data will undergo a conversion process and be transformed into the DL/T 698.45 protocol data frames [7, 8]. The transformation from the Modbus data format to the DL/T 698.45 protocol data format involves a series of intricate operations such as the decimal conversion of source data and target data, the

Table 1. Modbus Protocol Format and Data Types.

Content of the Statute	code naming	data type
address	Address	Unsigned char
function code	Funcontrol	enum
uplink error code	ERR	Unsigned char
Register Starting Address	register	struct
Data field length	nDatalen	Unsigned short
Data field content	Databuff	Unsigned char
check digit	CRC	struct

adjustment of precision, and the conversion of units. The converted data for the DL/T 698.45 protocol within the energy storage component encompasses a multitude of power parameters. A portion of the data conversions are presented in detail in the following Table 2:

Table 2. Energy storage protocol parameters and conversion ratios

Energy storage protocol parameters	unit (of measure)	conversion ratio
Cumulative charging capacity of energy storage	Kwh	1:1
Accumulated discharge power of energy storage	Kwh	1:1
total voltage	V	1:10
total current	A	1:10
SOC (State of Charge)	%	1:1
SOH (State of Health)	%	1:1
temp	°C	1:10

The plug-and-play mechanism founded on the Modbus protocol accomplishes the protocol adaptation of the distributed energy storage monitoring system. Its prominent advantage lies in its remarkable high flexibility and scalability. This method has the capability to automatically adjust the communication protocol and monitoring strategy in accordance with the distinct characteristics of different energy storage systems and their operating environments. By doing so, it ensures that the system remains in the optimal operating state at all times.

For example, in a large-scale commercial energy storage facility with multiple types and brands of equipment, this plug-and-play mechanism can seamlessly adapt the communication protocols to ensure efficient data transmission and monitoring.

Another instance could be a decentralized residential energy storage system where the mechanism adjusts the monitoring strategy based on the varying power consumption patterns of different households.

3 Communication Design for the Distributed Energy Storage Monitoring System

The distributed energy storage monitoring system is required to collect and monitor distributed power sources such as low-voltage photovoltaic inverters, energy storage devices, charging piles, etc. It supports high-speed dual-mode communication, namely the utilization of high-speed power line carrier communication (HPLC) and wireless communication (HRF). The communication protocols adhere to the requirements of the DL/T698.45 protocol and its extension regulations [9].

The uplink communication employs HPLC and wireless dual modes, and the communication protocol supports the DL/T698.45 protocol and its extension statute. The downstream communication utilizes RS-485, and the communication protocol accommodates the Modbus protocol of different PV inverter manufacturers.

3.1 Communication with Acquisition Terminals

The collection terminal undertakes operations such as parameter setting, data reading, and system regulation via the data transmission channel. The monitoring system facilitates the active reporting of relevant information to the collection terminal.

3.2 Communication with Circuit Breakers

The monitoring system interacts with the circuit breaker via RS-485 communication. Simultaneously, it supports the forwarding of interactive commands among the master station, collection terminal, and circuit breaker.

3.3 Communication with PV Inverters, Energy Storage, Charging Piles

The monitoring system communicates with PV inverters, charging piles, and other energy storage devices through RS-485, CAN, and other communication approaches.

This seamless communication and interaction framework lays a solid foundation for achieving intelligent energy management and control. It allows for real-time monitoring and adjustment of energy flow, ensuring optimal utilization and distribution of resources.

4   Designs of the Distributed Energy Storage Monitoring System

The designs of the distributed energy storage monitoring system is based on several core design ideas and principles. First of all, considering the variety of distributed energy storage systems, yet their functions are more consistent. The distributed energy storage monitoring system adopts a modular design concept, along with a plug-and-play mechanism to facilitate flexible configuration and expansion in accordance with different energy storage equipment scenarios. Secondly, to ensure real-time monitoring and accuracy, it is necessary for the energy storage monitoring module to collaborate with the fusion terminal to obtain the real-time operational status and performance data of the energy storage equipment, thereby conducting accurate analysis and prediction [7, 10–13].

The hardware of the system is developed based on a high-performance chip platform, which integrates metering, Bluetooth, dual-mode, carrier and other functions. Other components include memory, clock, reset and power management, security devices supporting boot loader signature verification, and peripheral interfaces supporting Ethernet controller, I2C interface, UART interface, SPI interface, GPIO interface and so on.

At the software level, the distributed energy storage monitoring module is divided into two layers: the operating system layer and the application layer. The operating system layer comprises the operating system kernel, system components, I/O device models, and other indispensable elements. The operating system provides the system call interface for the application layer through the system interface and accesses the hardware interface via the I/O device management interface.

The software application layer employs a multi-threaded design according to functional modules, including an uplink DL/T698.45 protocol communication protocol processing thread, a downlink energy storage communication protocol processing thread, a power metering processing thread, and a communication mode between threads that utilizes message queues and mailboxes. The software application layer thread design and communication flow is shown in Fig. 1:

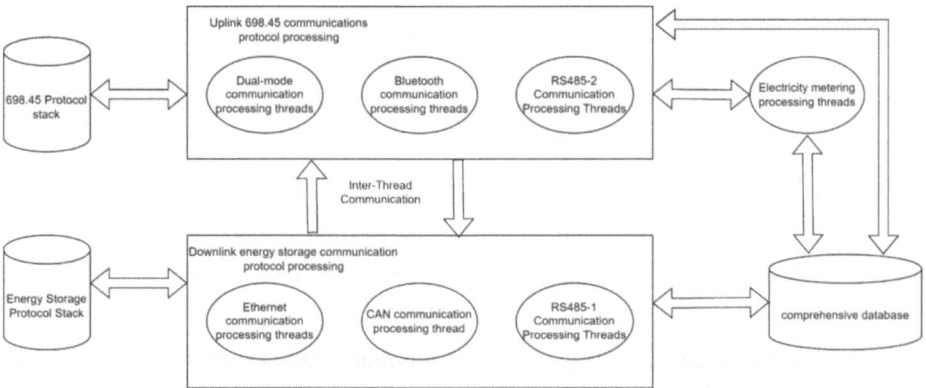

Fig. 1. Designs of Software Application Thread and Communication.

The detailed steps of the uplink DL/T698.45 protocol communication protocol processing flow are clearly illustrated in Fig. 2, providing a comprehensive overview for further understanding and analysis.

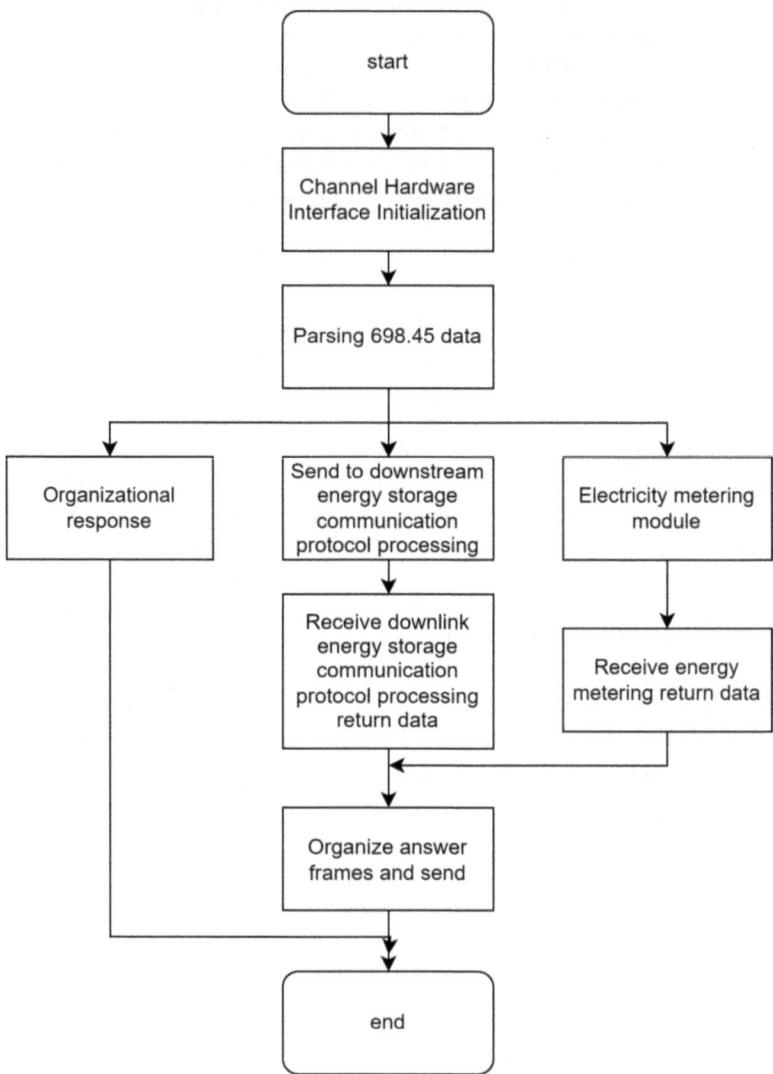

Fig. 2. Communication Processing of Uplink DL/T698.45 Protocol.

The downstream energy storage protocol communication processing flow is shown in Fig. 3, offering a detailed visual representation for better comprehension.

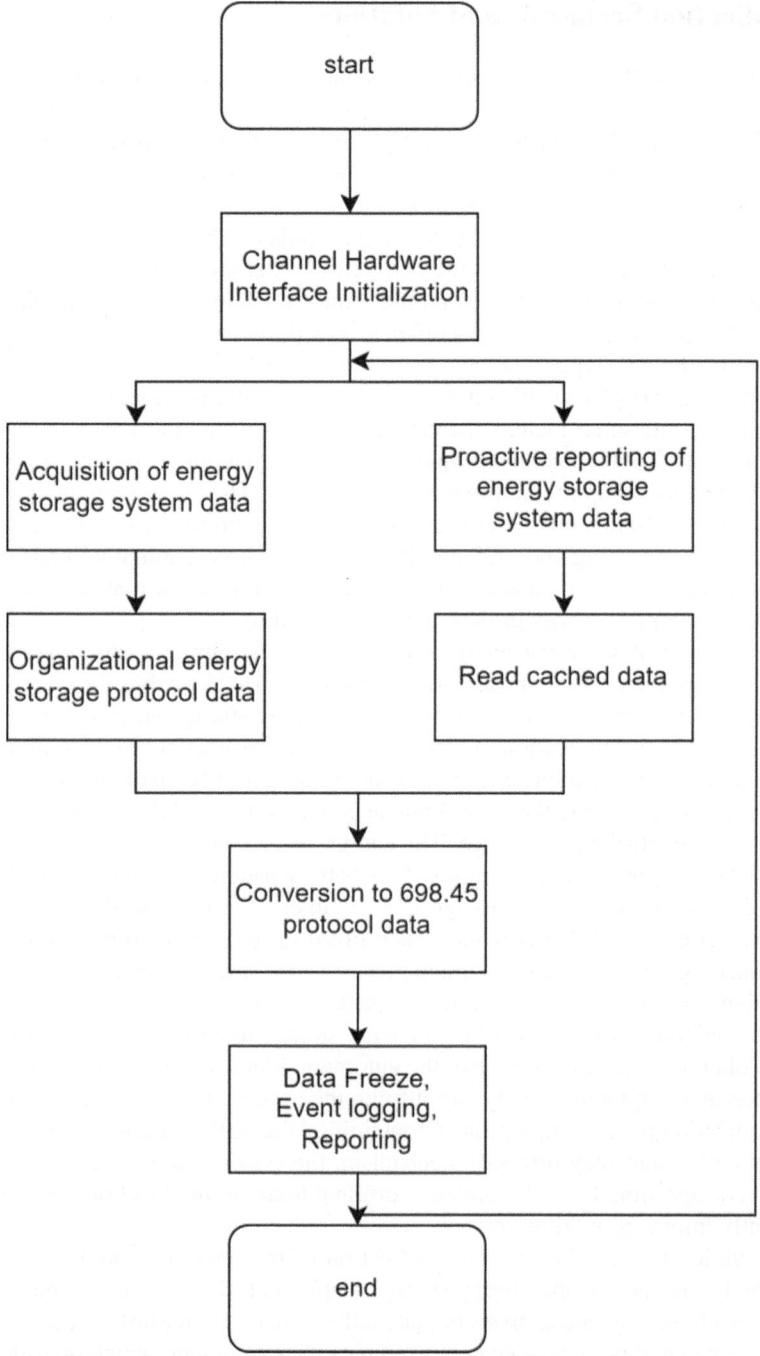

Fig. 3. Communication Processing of Downstream Energy Storage Protocol.

5 Application Scenarios and Solutions

In the existing distributed energy storage scenarios, the energy storage power station has not yet accomplished the perception and monitoring of its operational state. It is commonly achieved through the AC energy meter, which is utilized to measure the energy discharge from the storage station. The distribution network is incapable of sensing the subsequent connection of a storage station, and the energy storage and distribution network lack an interconnection mechanism. This gives rise to a deficiency in synergy and interaction between the two networks, along with an inadequate ability to regulate energy storage. Furthermore, the technical means for digital monitoring and operation of energy storage are not yet efficient, and the management level is insufficient. Consequently, the new type of storage regulation role is not yet played appropriately.

For the scenario of new PV energy storage users, the energy storage monitoring module replaces the smart meter to achieve energy storage monitoring. Simultaneously, with the perception of the fusion terminal, it realizes the panoramic monitoring of energy storage, as well as group regulation and group control. The energy storage monitoring module is plug-and-play, possesses the protocol conversion function, and has the capabilities of power metering and PCS monitoring. The fusion terminal unit has the functions of edge computing, data acquisition, analysis and decision-making, main station coordination, and pure energy grid-connected scheduling.

In the context of stock PV energy storage users, the aim is to minimize the alterations needed for the existing installation equipment. To achieve this, the energy storage monitoring module can be connected to the PV energy storage all-in-one machine via the RS485/CAN communication line, thereby enabling energy storage monitoring. The specific modification solution is depicted in Fig. 4. The Photovoltaic energy storage integrated machine, namely the energy management system (EMS), is a system utilized to monitor and control energy usage. The energy storage converter (PCS) is employed to control the charging and discharging of the battery pack and AC/DC conversion. The household photovoltaic energy storage EMS is integrated into the PCS of the energy storage converter. The AC energy meter is utilized for bidirectional metering of charging and discharging in the energy storage plant. The DC energy meter is used to monitor the charging and discharging of the battery pack.

In the implementation of distributed energy storage monitoring system, through the plug-and-play mechanism can realize the automatic identification and configuration of energy storage equipment, greatly simplifying the access process of equipment. In the actual application process, in a project containing 50 distributed energy storage nodes, through the plug-and-play protocol mechanism, the system successfully shortened the equipment access time from the project's original hours to the level of minutes, which significantly improved work efficiency.

Meanwhile, through the real-time collection of the operating status, power information, and fault data of the energy storage equipment via the convergence terminal, combined with the big data analysis on the platform side, it is feasible to accurately predict the lifespan and performance decay trend of the equipment, which provides strong support for the maintenance and management of the equipment. For instance, in a wind power energy storage project, the system successfully predicted that the life of a specific energy storage device would expire shortly by analyzing the equipment operation data.

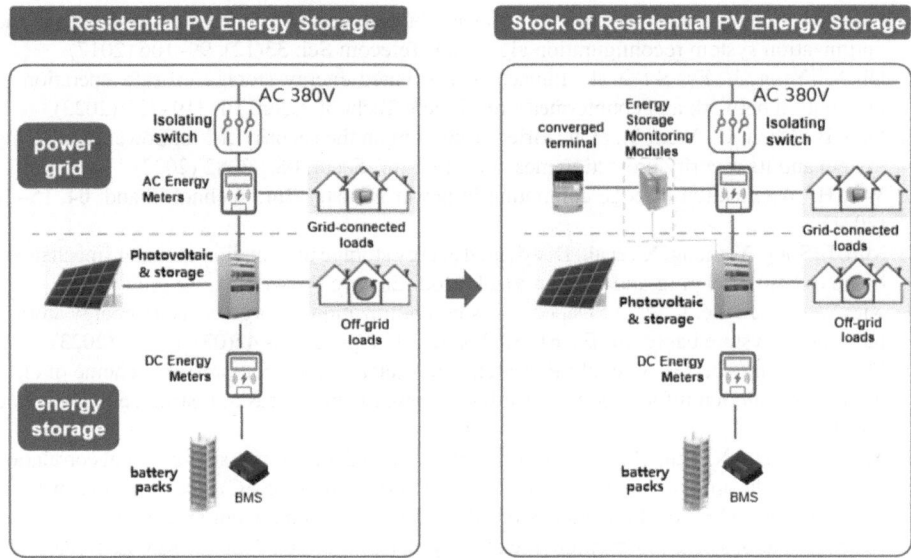

Fig. 4. Stock user energy storage monitoring and retrofitting program.

This enabled the replacement of the device in advance, thereby avoiding the loss of energy due to equipment failure.

6   Conclusions

The plug-and-play mechanism is proposed based on the Modus protocol, which improves the energy storage-related protocols at the protocol parsing and protocol adaptation layers.

The communication network of the distributed energy storage monitoring system is designed based on the plug-and-play mechanism, and the upstream and downstream protocol processing flow is described in detail. The protocol conversion and communication capabilities enable the system to interact with inverters from various brands and models.

As an illustrative example, the PV energy storage power station presents an energy storage monitoring program for both storage users and new users. This program, in conjunction with the fusion terminal, facilitates the opening of the energy storage and distribution network IOT and the implementation of panoramic monitoring of energy storage, group regulation, and group control.

References

1. Hou, Q., Peng, K., Dong, X., et al.: Design and implementation of monitoring system for new power system. Inf. Technol. Res. **49**(06), 52–59 (2023)
2. Jiang, L., Wang, H., Zhang, T., et al.: Design and implementation of intelligent energy storage system. Electron. Test. **36**(17) (2022)

3. Zang, Z., Zheng, P., Wei, B., et al.: Distribution network reliability assessment and optimization system reconfiguration algorithm. Telecom Sci. **33**(12), 99–106 (2017)
4. Qi, X., Yang, J., Fu, S., et al.: Impact of distributed energy storage on safe operation of distribution network and countermeasures. Electr. Technol. Econ. **10**, 319–322 (2023)
5. Guo, B., Chen, C., Wen, Y., et al.: Brief discussion on the security risk of power monitoring system and its security protection measures. Ind. Inf. Secur. **06**, 73–82 (2022)
6. Wei, H.: Application of edge computing in power industry. Inf. Technol. Stand. **04**, 15–21 (2021)
7. Min, J., Song, Y., Jiang, X., et al.: Distributed energy storage information exchange mechanism based on universal plug-and-play protocol. Mod. Electric Power 1–9
8. Xie, W., Ou, J., Ge, L., et al.: Data processing optimization of large-capacity energy storage monitoring system based on IEC 61850. Electrical Applications **42**(03), 69–75 (2023)
9. Dou, J., Zheng, G., Qi, S., et al.: Research on correlation data compression scheme of electricity consumption information acquisition system. Electric Measur. Instrum. **58**(10), 80–86 (2021)
10. Yao, D., Zhang, X., Sun, Z.: Research on application of data compression in signal correlation processing, the international society for applied computing (ISAC), the technical institute for engineers (TIE). In: Proceedings of 2021 2nd International Conference on Electronics, Communications and Information Technology (CECIT 2021).National Key Laboratory on Blind Signal Processing (2021)
11. Huang, Y., Huang, B.: Adaptive conversion system of access protocol for massive IoT devices based on data fusion. Electron. Des. Engi. **31**(10), 64–68 (2023)
12. Fan, W.: Application of information technology in control and management of distributed energy storage system. Coal Qual. Technol. **39**(01), 34–40 (2024)
13. Chen, S., Zhang, R., Nie, J.: Research on multi-protocol adaptive access method for heterogeneous devices. Autom. Expo **41**(04), 66–69 (2024)

Long Term Traffic Congestion Detection Method Based on Speed-Threshold

Mustapha Abubakar Ahmed, Azizul Rahman Mohd Shariff[(✉)],
and Saadatu Abubakar

School of Computer Sciences, Universiti Sains Malaysia, USM, 11800 George Town,
Penang, Malaysia
{mustaphaahmed,saadatu}@student.usm.my, azizulrahman@usm.my

Abstract. Congestion is bane and a persistent issue, especially in cities. It results in longer travel times, more fuel usage, and environmental pollution. Congestion occurs when traffic flow exceeds road capacity, which causes speeds to drop significantly below "free flow" or average speeds. 5G V2X allows ITS stations to exchange PSSCH that contains CAM. CAM carries vital information such as GPS coordinates and speed. Using this vital CAM information, this study developed a speed-based method dependent on a pre-defined threshold to identify congestion on roads more accurately. Results from simulation using real vehicle traffic traces indicate better congestion detection performance. There are more false detections based on time-gap as the performance measure as compared to speed. The proposed speed-threshold method achieved over 75% better detection results as compared to MCDP for long-term congestion detection.

Keywords: Vehicle speed · traffic congestion · congestion detection · cooperative awareness messages

1 Introduction

One of the most pressing concerns confronting the world today is road traffic congestion, exacerbated by a significant increase in the number of vehicles on the road and rapid urbanization. These are the two biggest reasons for traffic congestion on metropolitan roadways, according to [1]. Other causes of traffic congestion include, but are not limited to, insufficient traffic capacity and substantial red-light delays. Congestion on the roads is a difficult problem in most urban areas, and it occurs when demand reaches or exceeds the current transportation network capacity [2]. Increased traffic flow has a direct effect on congestion. Road traffic congestion has an impact on economic production, making it a concern for urban mobility. Furthermore, it harms the environment [3] and slows personal mobility [4].

Sometimes, extending an existing road or constructing a new one might help reduce traffic congestion, although doing so is expensive and time consuming [5].

© The Author(s), under exclusive license to Springer Nature Switzerland AG 2025
S. Zhang and L.-J. Zhang (Eds.): SCF 2024 - ICIOT 2024, LNCS 15427, pp. 25–39, 2025.
https://doi.org/10.1007/978-3-031-77003-6_3

Nevertheless, building more roads may not always be the best approach to relieve traffic congestion due to political, geographical, financial, and environmental factors [6]. Congestion detection and identification are critical in order to deploy control and mitigation measures, which will assist save lives while also addressing economic and environmental challenges caused by traffic congestion. The evolution of ITS which stand for Intelligent Transportation System [7] enables vehicles to communicate with other vehicles and network nodes through V2X [8], for cooperation and awareness. In addition, IOT applications are now gaining access to embedded sensors/actuators, providing information such as trajectories for future processes [9].

Vehicle traffic traces are sequences of position coordinates (longitude and latitude of GPS signals), time stamps, speed, angle, and other data collected from each vehicle within a predetermined time frame. These traces are similar to data found in CAM messages defined by the ETSI standard [10]. CAM are periodic messages exchanged between vehicles and have broadcast intervals between 100 ms and 1000 ms. In 5G V2X [11], CAMs are exchanged by vehicles using link layer Physical Sidelink Shared Control Channel (PSSCH) messages. This research takes advantage of the coordinates contained in the vehicle traffic trace to develop a speed-threshold congestion detection method. Vehicle traffic traces are collected for every 1000 ms (1 s), and this is equivalent to CAM messages being broadcast by vehicles at the maximum interval of 1 s. The system analyses two successive traces and extracts the coordinates to determine the distance traversed by each vehicle, and then uses the distance and the time interval between them to calculate vehicle speed. The system will monitor congestion every second using a congestion speed threshold of 30 km/h, which translates to a vehicle movement of 8.33 m per second. The contribution of this research is to use free CAM messages to develop a speed threshold road traffic congestion detection method for road traffic congestion measurement.

The rest of the paper is organized as follows: Section 2 covers relevant research on traffic congestion detection. Section 3 outlines the approach employed in this study to detect congestion, whereas Section 4 covers the presentation, evaluation, and discussion of the results. Section 5 concludes the paper with a spotlight of future work.

2   Related Work

To effectively control and mitigate traffic congestion, a reliable road traffic congestion detection component is essential. It also makes it possible to implement systems that alert cars ahead of time when they are about to enter an already congested region, thus increasing traffic safety. Congestion detection is a mechanism that generally triggers congestion alleviation or control procedures. Though there is no commonly accepted definition of congestion [12]. Congestion can be defined from users' expectations and also from the transportation angle as when there are too many cars using a segment of the road at one time, which causes the speeds to be slower, sometimes much slower than they should be. The work in [13], defines congestion when demand reaches or exceeds the current transportation network capacity. Various detection systems have been developed in recent years for monitoring road traffic congestion.

Many studies on detecting traffic jams have been published in the literature; like [14], which utilising IOT devices, to develop a cloud based smart parking system to reduce congestion on campus.

Congestion detection methods can be classified into three categories based on the technology used: sensor-based, vehicular ad-hoc network-based, and vision-based approaches [15]. Vision-based congestion detection systems such as [16,17], developed a density estimation method based on camera images. Other research work that developed a congestion detection protocol using vision-based and vehicle counting system includes [18,19], while [17,20], apply machine learning on vision-based data for congestion detection. These studies commonly employ cameras (vision-based) surveillance systems, which have become particularly important in traffic monitoring due to their ability to provide more information. However, they misidentify traffic congestion because they are unable to cover wide regions and might not take into consideration variations in vehicle speed distributions or moving orientations. An additional constraint associated with vision-based congestion detection is that traffic estimation relies on data obtained from a given place, which may not offer a precise depiction of traffic conditions across longer roads.

Several studies that use V2X cooperative awareness communication to develop congestion detection algorithms have also been published in the literature. In V2X communication, vehicles periodically broadcast CAM messages to other neighbouring communication nodes like vehicles, roadside units, etc., for cooperative awareness. CAM messages contain the vehicle's kinematic information like speed, location (latitude, and longitude), position, angle, etc., which can be used to estimate road traffic conditions.

To detect congestion in massive data clusters, [21] developed a V2X Location-based routing algorithm with cluster-based flooding (LORA-CBF), in which congestion detection was achieved by calculating the average speed for each cluster. In [22] the authors developed a segment-based congestion detection system where the system works by segmenting highways; vehicles on each segment form a cluster, with the head responsible for collecting beacons and calculating the average speed and occupancy of the segment. This information is sent to RSU for prediction using a decision tree and a random forest. In [23] an RFID-based positioning system was utilized to record the vehicle's location and speed, which was then transmitted to the cluster head. The cluster head will utilise this data to calculate the average speed and density of each lane, as well as to estimate traffic flow using fuzzy logic. Using RFID to capture location is expensive to acquire for all vehicles.

Clustering algorithm was used in [24] to cluster and mine vehicle trajectories. Using the haversine formula, the distance covered by each cluster is calculated, which is used to calculate speed ($speed = d/t$). The average speed is compared with the threshold to determine congestion. The limitation of this work is that it is based on historical data and uses a trajectory cluster. Cluster-based congestion detection is not real-time and it takes time. Another issue is the formation of clusters, and selecting the cluster head is time-consuming.

The work in [25] segmented vehicle trajectories based on time-window to build a congestion detection technique that takes both space and time into account. The method identified a slow-moving cluster by utilizing vehicle density and speed over time. Trajectory segmentation and moving cluster detection are the foundation of the concept. Given that clustering of vehicles is required for congestion estimation and only slow-moving vehicles are considered, this strategy might not truly detect congestion. There is a need to consider all vehicles.

To monitor traffic congestion, [26] creates an expert system and employs data mining techniques for tracking incidents and traffic congestion. According to the speed that was retrieved from the GPS traces, the algorithm mapped the GPS traces onto a road map and assigned a traffic state to each segment of the road. This approach relies on speed retrieved from the GPS traces data, which may not accurately define vehicle movement orientation, as vehicle speed at one point may not be the same at another point. Also, this method is not a real-time method.

The authors in [27], developed a VANET-based congestion detection and notification scheme for urban expressways using a Doppler frequency ship method, which is used to estimate and differentiate traffic conditions for major and auxiliary roads. It also combines vehicular cooperation and human assistance to determine overall congestion degree and location. This Method require human assistance.

A distributed and cooperative congestion detection system broadcasts the road ID and congestion parameter to other vehicles, while each vehicle monitors its speed and compares it to a threshold to estimate local congestion. This was proposed in [28]. The work used vehicle speed data, rather than computing movement speed, which may indicate non-congestion at one location and congestion at another. Also, judgement is made base on the received information, which may not cover all the vehicles on the road.

The works in [29, 30] present approaches for density estimation to detect congestion. The approach employed a piecewise switched linear macroscopic traffic model to estimate traffic density. Lane and intersection-base congestion detection technique were developed by [31]. GPS trajectories were analysed at intersections to detect congestion for each turn. ABEONA is a beacon-based congestion monitoring and prediction protocol that was presented by [32]. A V2V congestion detection technique called ABEONA calculates density based on the quantity of cars on the road.

A congestion detection system (COTEC) based on density and speed was developed by [33]. Vehicle speed was computed, and density was estimated using the received beacons to measure congestion. The study used a fuzzy-logic-based approach with little overhead to identify, correlate, and estimate the level of congestion. The approach incurs overhead.

The work in [34] used the haversine formula; a floating-car dataset was utilized to calculate the distance travelled by each vehicle. The speed of each vehicle was then determined by utilising the distance over time. To track traffic, the speed was plotted on the roads. Though the paper calculated the speed based on the vehicle's journey distance, it failed to specify the time and the congestion threshold.

MCDP was proposed in [35], a framework in which each vehicle estimates the headway and time gap between neighbouring vehicles and counts the number of vehicles based on the beacon message it has received to detect congestion in the absence of infrastructure. If the time gap (Tg) is less than the designated safety threshold, congestion is detected. This study only tracks traffic jams that occur within a vehicle's transmission range; it might not be an accurate representation of larger traffic jams. Because of their speed, using intervehicle spacing may cause congestion when none exists.

According to [22], GPS-based congestion detection is the cheapest and most widely used method. With GPS-based congestion detection, large areas can be monitored, and vehicles can also be easily tracked. congestion can be measured using metrics like speed, travel time, density, congestion index, etc.

This work proposes a speed-threshold congestion detection system that uses vehicle trajectories in vehicle traces to calculate vehicle movement speed. Speed-threshold congestion detection provides a real-time and broader coverage for detecting road traffic congestion.

3 Methodology

In a vehicular environment, a node-to-node road network G can be represented as a collection of nodes (intersections) V connected by directed links (roads) R denoted as $G = (V, R)$. Each directed road $r_{mn} \in R$ from node v_m to node v_n where $v_{mn} \in V$ contains moving vehicles that allows vehicle traces to be collected. In 5G V2X, vehicles on any road broadcast PSSCH message that carries CAM containing multiple data traces, as shown in Fig. 1

Let $P = \{p_0, p_1, ..., p_j\}$ denote a road coordinate point, where $p_j = (Q_j, \lambda_j)$, Q_j is the latitude point, and λ_j is the longitude point. The position of the vehicle on the road at time t, when it is transmitting its CAM message, is known as the vehicle position (p). The vehicle leaves point p_i at time t_0 and arrives at point p_j at time t_1.

The vehicle ID (V_{IDi}), position coordinate, direction, speed, road ID, time stamp, and other data are included in the state information. The reference position, i.e., the longitude and latitude of every vehicle, is used in this work to determine the distance driven within $1s$. We define d as the distance between two consecutive coordinate points. To calculate d from GPS coordinates, the haversine formula (1) is used, as in [24]

$$d = 2r \arcsin(\sqrt{(hav(Q_2 - Q_1) + \cos(Q_1)\cos(Q_2) \, hav(\lambda_2 - \lambda_1))} \qquad (1)$$

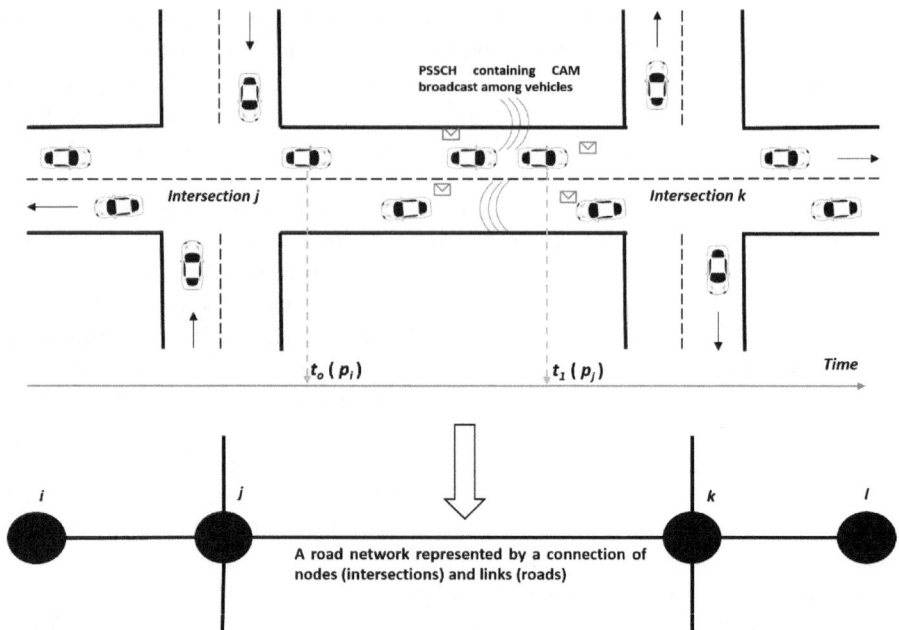

Fig. 1. Showing nodes (intersections), and edges (roads).

where d is the distance between two coordinate points, λ_1 and λ_2 are the longitudes of the two points, Q_1 and Q_2 are the latitudes of the two points, and r is the radius of the earth.

Vehicle speed (VS) can be calculated by dividing the distance travelled (d) by the time (t). The system will calculate the speed for each vehicle after every second. Equation (2) can be used to compute a vehicle's speed VS;

$$VS = d \div t \tag{2}$$

Congestion is regarded as occurring when the observed real-time traffic measure on a road exceeds a predefined threshold. To quantify congestion, researchers often develop a critical threshold for a variety of characteristics, such as travel time, speed, density, and road occupancy. One of the most important factors and the most often used metric for judging congestion is speed. In this research, a speed of 30 km/h equivalent to 8.33 m/s is set as a threshold. Using the threshold of 30 km/h, a vehicle will cover 8.33 m in one second (1 s), and the one-second (1 s) interval was driven from the fact that the maximum CAM transmission rate is 1 s. If the congestion value is less than 8.33 m/s, there is congestion; otherwise, there is no congestion.

Congestion found on a single road is referred to as **long-term** traffic congestion detection. The process of identifying congestion in a zone or collection of roads is known as **global** congestion detection. The two types of congestion detection are depicted in Fig. 2

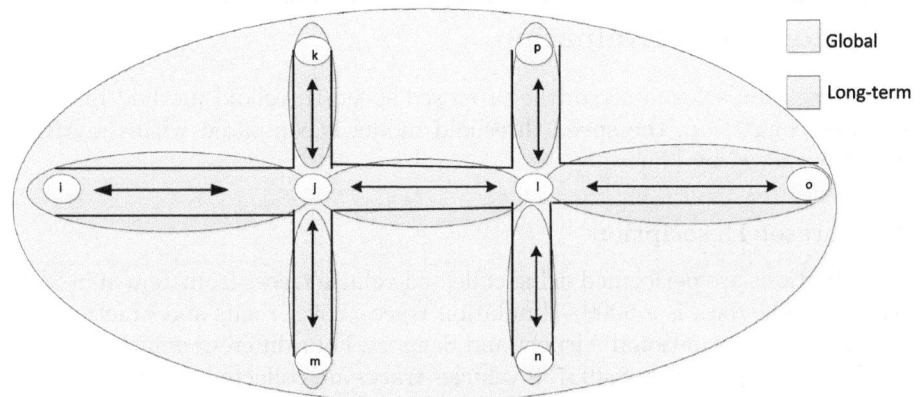

Fig. 2. Congestion detection levels.

3.1 Long-Term Traffic Congestion Detection

Long-term congestion detection involves the monitoring of traffic congestion on one single road. To compute long-term congestion, we consider a road r_{mn} of length L and, an N number of vehicles where $N = \{V_{ID1}, V_{ID2}, ...V_{IDk}\}$. Using the formula (3), we measure the long-term congestion (LC) of the road r_{mn} by computing the average VS of all vehicles traveling the road r_{mn} for a period of t.

$$LC_{r_{m,n}} = \frac{\sum_{k=1}^{N} VS_{IDk}}{N} \tag{3}$$

where LC is the average congestion level of the road $r_{m,n}$, VS is the vehicle speed of the vehicle IDk, and N is the total number of vehicles on the road $r_{m,n}$ at time t.

3.2 Global Congestion Detection

Global congestion detection is used to monitor road traffic congestion in a certain area or zone. In this paper, a zone, or region, is defined as an area with two or more roads. Consider a set of roads $R = (r_{1,2}, r_{2,3}, ..., r_{m,n})$ within a zone Z. The average traffic congestion of every road $r_{m,n}$ in the zone Z can be used to calculate the region's global congestion (GC). In other words, GC may refer to the aggregate of all LC of $r_{m,n}$ in Z. Formula (4) can be used to calculate the global congestion level for an area Z at time t.

$$GC_z = \frac{\sum LC_{r_{m,n}}}{R} \tag{4}$$

where GC_z is the global congestion measured for a region z. Global congestion detection enables traffic managers to broaden their understanding of congestion beyond a single roadway, as congestion spreads from one road to another.

4   Performance Evaluation

To measure the performance of the proposed speed-threshold method in detecting traffic congestion, the speed-threshold model is compared with the MCDP method proposed by [35]

4.1   Dataset Description

The evaluations are performed using collected vehicle traces from Jeju-si in South Korea [36]. The data is a 5000 s simulation traces, cover roads and junctions surrounding Jeju International Airport and Seaport. Four different vehicles type are simulated, approximately 8,495739 vehicles traces are collected, with each having the following information: vehicle-id, time, longitude, latitude, speed, position, type, angle, and lane-id. Six different roads are chosen namely Seogwang-ro, Doryeong-ro, Yeonsam-ro, Sindae-ro, Gonghang-ro and Gonghangseo-ro to measure the performances of global and long-term traffic congestion detection. The vehicles traces are validated and processed using the SUMO simulation, and models tested using Python-based Google Colab. Figure 3, shows the geographical map of the Jeju International Airport and Seaport area, and the specific roads where the vehicle traces are extracted.

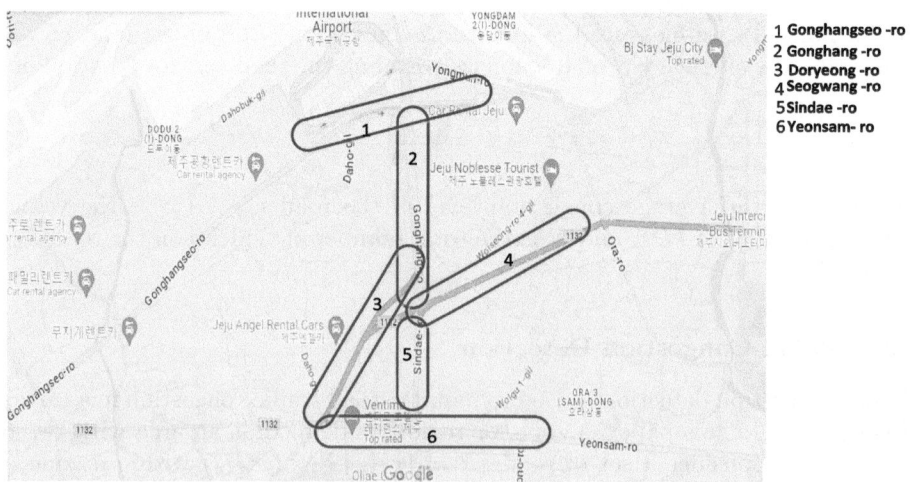

Fig. 3. Map showing roads where the vehicle traces are extracted.

4.2   Results Presentation and Analysis

Speed is one of the most important and widely used metrics for determining congestion. To better detect traffic congestion, as stated earlier, speed threshold of 30 km/h (8.33 m/s) was defined. A vehicle or a group of vehicles detected to travel below the pre-defined threshold is considered to be moving at congestion speed or is in a congestion situation. The MCDP instead uses a time headway of 2 s as the threshold. If the time headway is less than 2 s, congestion is said to occur.

Figure 4 depicts the average vehicle speed and average time headway of all vehicles traversing Gonghang-ro and Yeonsam-ro for speed-threshold and MCDP respectively, calculated every one second (1 s), for the simulation duration of 100 s. The results show that average vehicle speed is less than 8.33 m/s, indicating a crowded route for the whole duration of 100 s. Speed-threshold congestion detection outperforms time headway in detection of long-term congestion. According to the results, speed-threshold method detects congestion at every instant over time, whereas time headway did not capture congestion in 64 out of 83 instances (Table 1). MCDP reported only 22.89% congestion instances as compared to speed-threshold method. Ultimately, the results suggest that vehicles on this road (Gonghang-ro) are going at a very slow speed, indicating a congested road, which is understandable given the fact that the road is the main road linking to Jeju seaport and airport, which is one of the busiest airports in the world.

Table 1. Congestion detection comparison for Gonghang road and Yeonsam-ro (long-term).

	Gonghang-ro	Yeonsam-ro
Speed-Based	83	47
MCDP	19	77

Congestion detection results for Yeonsam-ro in Fig. 4 indicates false detection instances for MCDP as compared to speed-threshold. Speed-threshold method is able to track congestion build-ups and detect congestions more reliably. Despite reporting 77 detections (Table 1), not all of the congestion instances detected for MCDP are accurate. There are 30 inaccurate detection instances captured by MCDP, which is 38.96% higher than speed-threshold method. This results clearly revealed that time headway is not suitable for congestion detection since it cannot detect congestion even when the vehicle speeds are high. As seen in Fig. 4 results, as the simulation period increases, the number of vehicles will increase, hence vehicle speed decreases. The reduction in average vehicle speed generally indicates congestion or congestion build-up. In this situation, speed threshold is able to distinguish between congestion and non-congestion more accurately since vehicle speed is inversely related to vehicle density.

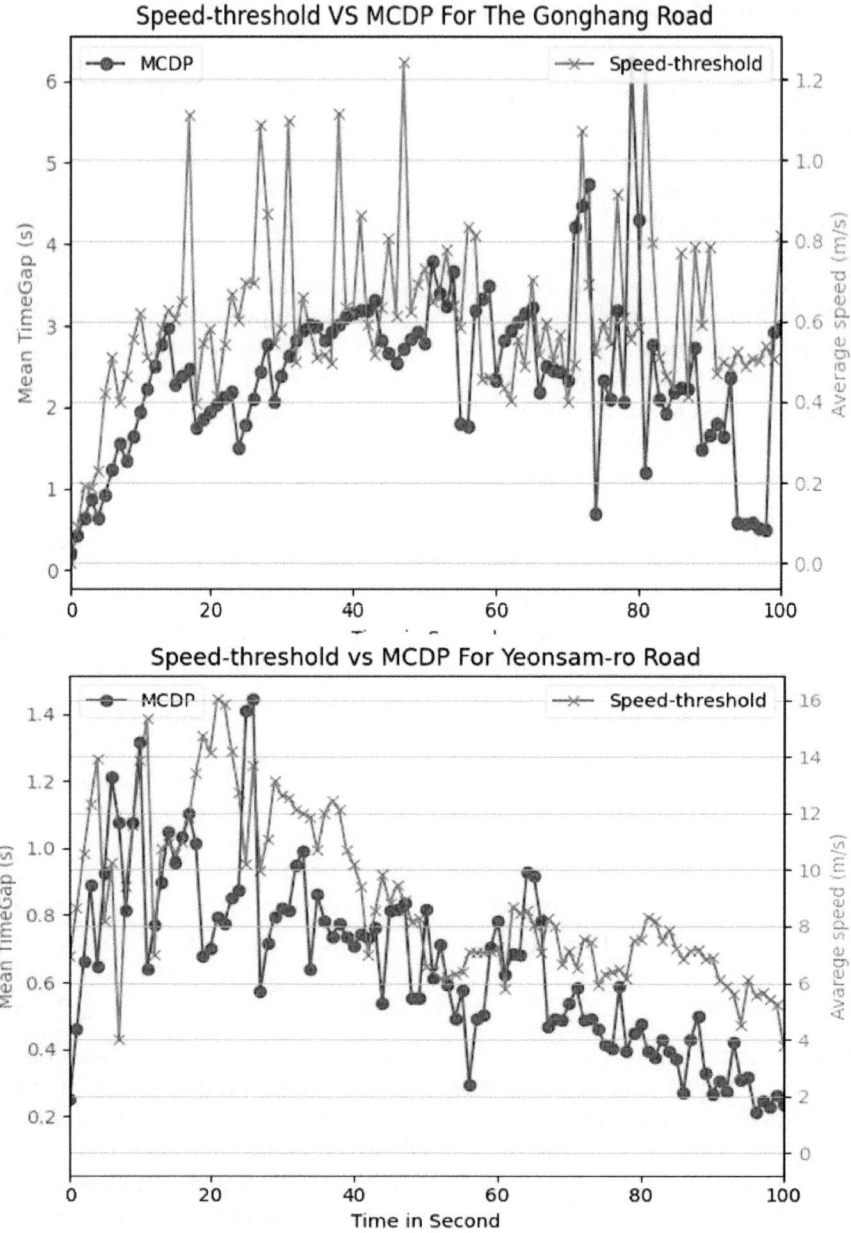

Fig. 4. Speed-threshold vs MCDP result for Gonghang-ro and Yeonsam-ro road (long-term).

Drivers in congested locations are more inclined to allow space between them out of fear of possible accidents, resulting in longer time-headway. While in free-flow traffic conditions, drivers are not very attentive with the spacing between them, because there are not many vehicles on the road and they do not expect to encounter sudden braking while speeding. Hence, time-headway is not suitable for congestion detection. In these free-flow traffic, vehicle spacing or time headway being kept by drivers are also very erratic, hence potentially causing inaccurate detections and of congestion by the MCDP method.

The results and arguments above are supported by the results in Fig. 5. Several vehicles movement are recorded individually from the start until the end of the journey. The vehicle speeds and relative time-gaps specifically are measured. Vehicles with the ID of Jps730, Jps744, JTs754 shows a travelling speed above the threshold of 8.33 m/s, indication of non-congested situation for the speed threshold method. However, for the MCDP method, these vehicles exhibited a time headway below 2 s, which falsely exhibits a congestion situation. Speed is a better measure of congestion as compared to time-gap in MCDP, and having a realistic speed threshold to measure congestion makes detection more accurate.

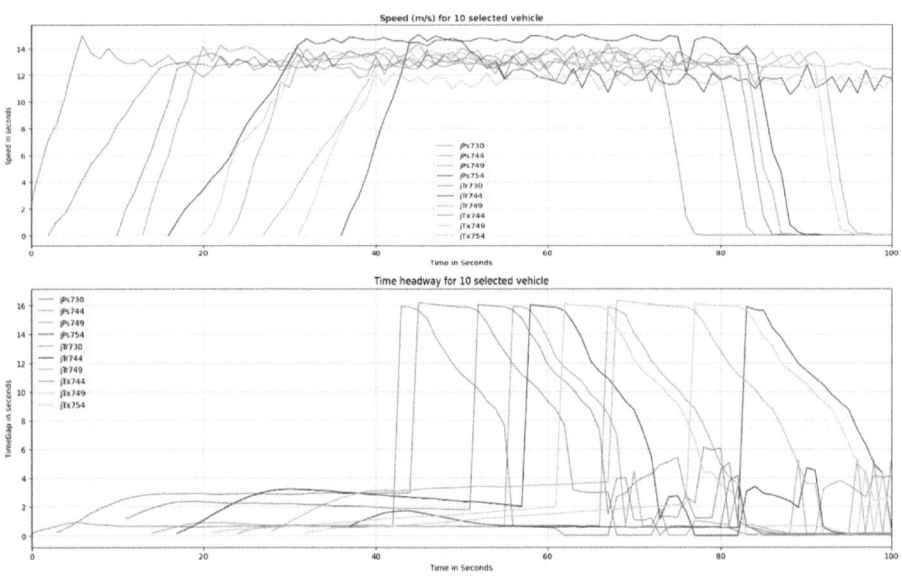

Fig. 5. Speed-threshold vs MCDP result for 10 selected vehicles.

A combined result of the average speed-threshold and time headway for global congestion detection is presented in Fig. 6. The results demonstrate that the average vehicle speed on the roads fluctuates over time, and speed-threshold method is able to detect congestion more precisely. It captures instances of non-congestion between the time window of 25 s and 70 s. In contrast for MCDP using time headway as the measure, the result shows the average time headway is less than 2 s throughout the 100-seconds period, indicating persistent false congestion on all of the roads examined. Speed-threshold is able to detect congestion in 78 instances, representing 82.98% of 94 recorded by MCDP. While MCDP detects congestion in all the instances, i.e., 94, representing 17.02% higher than speed-threshold (Table 2).

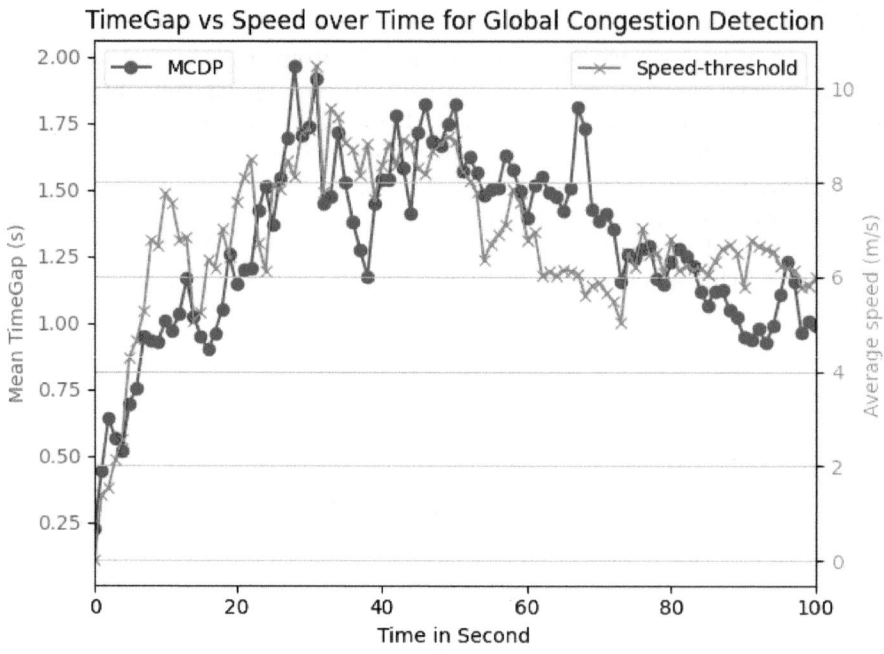

Fig. 6. Speed-threshold vs MCDP result for global congestion detection

Table 2. Congestion detection comparison for global congestion detection.

	Detection Point
Speed-Based	78
MCDP	94

In comparative analysis, it was empirically shown that under conditions of minimal traffic flow, the speed-threshold method did not detect congestion, whereas the MCDP method exhibited sensitivity to congestion even under low traffic conditions. As traffic volume increase over time, the average speed declined below the threshold indicative of congestion in the speed-threshold method, whereas the MCDP method maintained a consistent behaviour without significant variation even as traffic density increases. In a global environment, not all roads are crowded; therefore, the average speed of all roads at a time may result in non-congestion due to the effect of non-congested roads. With time headway, the inter-vehicle distance may be below the threshold of 2 s, even though the vehicles are moving slowly.

5 Conclusion and Future Work

Cooperative awareness technology such as 5G V2X for vehicles offers potential advanced solutions to road traffic management in distant future. Using CAM messages exchanged between vehicles, the temporal free information contained in CAM specifically vehicle ID, GPS coordinates and vehicle speed can be captured by road side ITS stations to measure the level of traffic congestion accurately.

This research developed a speed-threshold congestion detection system based on a predefined speed threshold of 30 km/h, or 8.33 m/s. This speed threshold determines road traffic congestion, with vehicle movement speeds calculated from traffic traces. Instead of relying on a single point speed, this method enables for the precise capturing of a vehicle's travel along any given road over time. Two simple and implementable congestion detection schemes are proposed, which are the long-term and global traffic detection and their performance against MCDP have been investigated. Results show that the speed-threshold method outperforms MCDP in its ability to capture accurately congestion instances. There are more false congestion detection for MCDP using time-headway as its performance measure. Time-headway is not a good measure because its parameters fluctuates partly not because the speed factor, but rather due to some erratic decisions by drivers. There are tendencies for drivers to maintain large gaps in congestion situations to avoid rear-end collisions, and smaller gaps can also be seen kept by drivers on some highways. These factors eventually prohibit time-headway from being the better measure to detect congestion.

The speed-threshold method provides an effective technique for detecting traffic congestion. As stated in the literature, integrating two or more congestion detection measures can improve detection accuracy. In the future, speed thresholds will be combined with additional parameter to improve its accuracy.

References

1. Rizwan, P., Suresh, K., Babu, M.R.: Real-time smart traffic management system for smart cities by using Internet of Things and big data. In: 2016 International Conference on Emerging Technological Trends (ICETT), pp. 1–7. IEEE (2016)
2. Chong, H.F., Ng, D.W.K.: Development of IoT device for traffic management system. In: 2016 IEEE Student Conference on Research and Development (SCOReD), pp. 1–6. IEEE (2016)
3. Falcocchio, J.C., Levinson, H.S.: Road traffic congestion: a concise guide. Springer Tracts Transp. Traffic **7**, 159–182 (2015)
4. Joshi, Y., Joshi, A., Tayade, N., Shinde, P., Rokade, S.M.: IoT based smart traffic density alarming indicator. Int. Res. J. Eng. Technol. **3**(10), 1086–1089 (2016)

5. Zhou, Z., Lin, S., Xi, Y.: A fast network partition method for large-scale urban traffic networks. J. Control Theory Appl. **11**(3), 359–366 (2013)
6. Ibáñez, J.A.G., Zeadally, S., Contreras-Castillo, J.: Integration challenges of intelligent transportation systems with connected vehicle, cloud computing, and Internet of Things technologies. IEEE Wirel. Commun. **22**(6), 122–128 (2015)
7. Dimitrakopoulos, G., Demestichas, P.: Intelligent transportation systems: systems based on cognitive networking principles and management functionality. IEEE Veh. Technol. Mag. **5**(1), 77–84 (2010)
8. Cinque, E., Persia, F.A., Chiocchio, S., Santucci, F., Pratesi, M.: V2X communication technologies and service requirements for connected and autonomous driving. In: AEIT International Conference of Electrical and Electronic Technologies for Automotive, AEIT AUTOMOTIVE 2020, pp. 2–7 (2020)
9. Gomes, R., Bouloukakis, G., Costa, F., Georgantas, N., da Rocha, R.: QoS-aware resource allocation for mobile IoT Pub/Sub systems. In: Georgakopoulos, D., Zhang, L.-J. (eds.) ICIOT 2018. LNCS, vol. 10972, pp. 70–87. Springer, Cham (2018). https://doi.org/10.1007/978-3-319-94370-1_6
10. ETSI: Vehicular Communications; Basic Set of Applications; Part 2: Specification of Cooperative, vol. 1. ETSI Standard (2010)
11. Alalewi, A., Dayoub, I., Cherkaoui, S.: On 5G–V2X use cases and enabling technologies: a comprehensive survey. IEEE Access **2021**(9), 107710–107737 (2021)
12. Toan, T.D., Wong, Y.D.: Fuzzy logic-based methodology for quantification of traffic congestion. Phys. A **570**, 125784 (2021)
13. Ho, M.C., Lim, J.M.Y., Soon, K.L., Chong, C.Y.: An improved pheromone-based vehicle rerouting system to reduce traffic congestion. Appl. Soft Comput. **84**, 105702 (2019)
14. Alsbou, N., Afify, M., Ali, I.: Cloud-based IoT smart parking system for minimum parking delays on campus. In: Issarny, V., Palanisamy, B., Zhang, L.-J. (eds.) ICIOT 2019. LNCS, vol. 11519, pp. 131–139. Springer, Cham (2019). https://doi.org/10.1007/978-3-030-23357-0_11
15. Chetouane, A., Mabrouk, S., Mosbah, M.: Traffic congestion detection: solutions, open issues and challenges. In: Jemili, I., Mosbah, M. (eds.) DiCES-N 2020. CCIS, vol. 1348, pp. 3–22. Springer, Cham (2020). https://doi.org/10.1007/978-3-030-65810-6_1
16. Lam, C.T., Gao, H., Ng, B.: A real-time traffic congestion detection system using on-line images. In: 2017 IEEE 17th International Conference on Communication Technology (ICCT), pp. 1548–1552. IEEE, October 2017
17. Sonnleitner, E., Barth, O., Palmanshofer, A., Kurz, M.: Traffic measurement and congestion detection based on real-time highway video data. Appl. Sci. **10**(18), 6270 (2020)
18. Liu, F., Zeng, Z., Jiang, R.: A video-based real-time adaptive vehicle-counting system for urban roads. PLoS ONE **12**(11), e0186098 (2017)
19. Song, H., Liang, H., Li, H., Dai, Z., Yun, X.: Vision-based vehicle detection and counting system using deep learning in highway scenes. Eur. Transp. Res. Rev. **11**(1), 1–16 (2019). https://doi.org/10.1186/s12544-019-0390-4
20. Kurniawan, J., Syahra, S.G., Dewa, C.K.: Traffic congestion detection: learning from CCTV monitoring images using convolutional neural network. Procedia Comput. Sci. **144**, 291–297 (2018)
21. Cárdenas-Benítez, N., Aquino-Santos, R., Magaña-Espinoza, P., Aguilar-Velazco, J., Edwards-Block, A., Medina Cass, A.: Traffic congestion detection system through connected vehicles and big data. Sensors **16**(5), 599 (2016)

22. Alnami, H.M., Mahgoub, I., Al-Najada, H.: Segment based highway traffic flow prediction in VANET using big data analysis. In: 2021 IEEE Symposium Series on Computational Intelligence (SSCI), pp. 01–08. IEEE, December 2021
23. Zhang, E.Z., Zhang, X.: Road traffic congestion detecting by VANETs. In: 2nd International Conference on Electrical and Electronic Engineering (EEE 2019), pp. 242–248. Atlantis Press, July 2019
24. Chaurasia, B.K., Manjoro, W.S., Dhakar, M.: Traffic congestion identification and reduction. Wireless Pers. Commun. **114**(2), 1267–1286 (2020)
25. Shi, Y., Wang, D., Tang, J., Deng, M., Liu, H., Liu, B.: Detecting spatiotemporal extents of traffic congestion: a density-based moving object clustering approach. Int. J. Geogr. Inf. Sci. **35**(7), 1449–1473 (2021)
26. D'Andrea, E., Marcelloni, F.: Detection of traffic congestion and incidents from GPS trace analysis. Expert Syst. Appl. **73**, 43–56 (2017)
27. Yuan, Q., Liu, Z., Li, J., Zhang, J., Yang, F.: A traffic congestion detection and information dissemination scheme for urban expressways using vehicular networks. Transp. Res. Part C: Emerg. Technol. **47**(2), 114–127 (2014)
28. Milojevic, M., Rakocevic, V.: Short paper distributed vehicular traffic congestion detection algorithm for urban environments. In: 2013 IEEE Vehicular Networking Conference, pp. 182–185. IEEE, December 2013
29. Harrou, F., Zeroual, A., Sun, Y.: Traffic congestion monitoring using an improved kNN strategy. Measurement **156**, 107534 (2020)
30. Zeroual, A., Harrou, F., Sun, Y.: Road traffic density estimation and congestion detection with a hybrid observer-based strategy. Sustain. Urban Areas **46**, 101411 (2019)
31. Kan, Z., Tang, L., Kwan, M.P., Ren, C., Liu, D., Li, Q.: Traffic congestion analysis at the turn level using Taxis' GPS trajectory data. Comput. Environ. Urban Syst. **74**, 229–243 (2019)
32. Gramaglia, M., Calderon, M., Bernardos, C.J.: ABEONA monitored traffic: VANET-assisted cooperative traffic congestion forecasting. IEEE Veh. Technol. Mag. **9**(2), 50–57 (2014)
33. Bauza, R., Gozálvez, J.: Traffic congestion detection in large-scale scenarios using vehicle-to-vehicle communications. J. Netw. Comput. Appl. **36**(5), 1295–1307 (2013)
34. Yong-chuan, Z., Xiao-qing, Z., Zhen-ting, C.: Traffic congestion detection based on GPS floating-car data. Procedia Eng. **15**, 5541–5546 (2011)
35. Ahmad, M., Chen, Q., Khan, Z.: Microscopic congestion detection protocol in VANETs. J. Adv. Transp. **2018**(1), 6387063 (2018)
36. Mehmood, A., Mehmood, F.: Vehicular trajectories from Jeju, South Korea. IEEE Dataport (2022). https://doi.org/10.21227/y8vk-wj40

Application of Digital Exhibition and Preservation of Intangible Cultural Heritage via Holographic Real-Time Cloud Broadcasting

Xuejiao Pang⑩, Shujin Li⑩, Yiying Jiang, Shun Zhang⑩, Mingmin Gong, and Xiaohu Fan⁽✉⁾ ⑩

Wuhan Collage, 333# Huangjiahu Road, Wuhan 430070, Hubei, China
{9452,9093,9420}@whxy.edu.cn, {23201190209,23201180134, 23201190314}@mail.whxy.edu.cn

Abstract. This paper introduces a pioneering technological framework integrating holographic real-time cloud broadcasting for the digital preservation and exhibition of intangible cultural heritage (ICH). The framework, adaptable to diverse cultural elements, ensures accurate digitization and immersive presentation, facilitating global access and cultural education. Through high-resolution scanning, sophisticated data processing, and cloud-based broadcasting, the system delivers real-time holographic content. User interaction is enhanced through gesture recognition and multi-sensory feedback, promoting an engaging and educational experience. The paper also addresses challenges such as data security and cultural authenticity, proposing solutions like end-to-end encryption and context-aware algorithms. Case studies illustrate the framework's successful application in traditional crafts and music, highlighting its potential for sustainable cultural heritage preservation.

Keywords: Intangible Cultural Heritage (ICH) · Holographic Real-time Cloud Broadcasting · Digital Preservation · Cultural Education and Accessibility

1 Introduction

1.1 Research Background

In the era of globalization and digital information, intangible cultural heritage (ICH) faces the dilemma of inheritance and dissemination [1]. Globalization, a double-edged sword, facilitates the exchange of diverse cultural achievements while simultaneously posing challenges to the survival and development of local cultures. As stated in the "Action Plan for Cultural Policy Development," the competition in cultural productivity is set to become a primary battlefield in the future world, and cultural development will be the mainstream of new era social progress. The advent of an era integrating culture and technology presents both opportunities and challenges for the protection of ICH [2]. Against this backdrop, holographic real-time cloud broadcasting technology offers new possibilities for the digital preservation of ICH [3].

© The Author(s), under exclusive license to Springer Nature Switzerland AG 2025
S. Zhang and L.-J. Zhang (Eds.): SCF 2024 - ICIOT 2024, LNCS 15427, pp. 40–52, 2025.
https://doi.org/10.1007/978-3-031-77003-6_4

1.2 Motivation

This study aims to explore and apply holographic real-time cloud broadcasting technology to provide innovative pathways for the digital preservation, inheritance, and exhibition of intangible cultural heritage.

Firstly, applying holographic real-time cloud broadcasting technology to ICH protection in the context of globalization has significant practical implications. This technology can effectively address issues such as the extensive geographical distribution of ICH and the aging of inheritors, while also enhancing the appeal and influence of ICH, promoting its sustainable development.

Secondly, the theoretical integration of holographic real-time cloud broadcasting technology with ICH protection holds academic value, contributing to the enrichment of the intersection between holographic technology and cultural integration.

Thirdly, comparative and case studies that clarify the current state of technological application in ICH protection in China, analyze existing problems, and propose countermeasures, offer constructive significance in addressing these issues.

1.3 Research Methods

This research will employ a multifaceted approach, including literature review, case analysis, and technical research. It will synthesize the current state of research and technological development trends both domestically and internationally to explore the potential and implementation pathways of holographic real-time cloud broadcasting technology in ICH protection.

2 Related Works

The intersection of holographic technology and cultural heritage has emerged as a pioneering field, offering innovative solutions for the digital preservation and exhibition of ICH [1]. This chapter reviews the scholarly and technological landscape, highlighting key practices and assessing their merits and limitations.

2.1 Holographic Display Technologies

Holographic display technologies have seen significant advancements, transitioning from early laser-based systems to modern digital projection methods. The evolution of these technologies has been well-documented in various academic circles. For instance, research by Zhang et al. [4] explores the application of holographic displays in museum exhibits, emphasizing the enhanced viewer engagement and educational value.

2.2 Real-Time Data Processing and Cloud Broadcasting

The integration of real-time data processing with cloud broadcasting has been crucial for the live streaming and remote access of holographic content. Smith and Johnson [5] provide an in-depth analysis of cloud computing's role in facilitating real-time holographic transmission, underscoring the improvements in data handling and reduced latency.

2.3   Digital Preservation of ICH

Digital preservation strategies for ICH have been extensively studied, with a focus on the accuracy of digital replication and the long-term storage of cultural data. A seminal work by **Kumar and Lee** [6] discusses the use of 3D scanning and photogrammetry for the accurate digitization of cultural artifacts, highlighting both the technical precision and the challenges of color reproduction and texture preservation.

2.4   Immersive Experiences and Virtual Reality

The use of virtual reality (VR) in conjunction with holographic technology has opened new avenues for immersive experiences of ICH. **Williams** [7] examines VR's potential to simulate traditional performances and rituals, providing a more profound connection to the cultural context.

2.5   Challenges and Limitations

Despite the technological advancements, several challenges persist. The high cost of holographic equipment, as discussed by **Foster** [8], can limit widespread adoption, especially in developing regions with rich cultural heritages. Additionally, **Sato and Gaoaddress** the issue of preserving the authenticity of ICH in digital formats, noting the risk of information loss and misinterpretation [9].

2.6   Academic and Technological Approaches

Academic research has primarily focused on the theoretical underpinnings and ethical considerations of digital ICH preservation. In contrast, technological approaches have prioritized practical implementation, user experience, and system interoperability. A comparative study by **Chen et al.** [10] evaluates different digital preservation methods, weighing the trade-offs between technological feasibility and cultural fidelity.

The review of related works reveals a dynamic field where technological innovation and academic inquiry are synergistically advancing the frontiers of ICH preservation. While the benefits of holographic technology in creating immersive and accessible cultural experiences are evident, the challenges of cost, authenticity, and technological accessibility require further attention [11].

3   Framework and Implementation

The chapter delves into the intricate architecture of our proposed system, a harmonious fusion of theoretical constructs and practical technological implementations, designed to encapsulate the digital essence of ICH.

3.1 System Architecture

At the core of our framework is a robust, four-tiered architecture meticulously engineered to address the complex requirements of ICH digitization. The architecture comprises the following layers (Fig. 1):

Data Acquisition Layer: This foundational layer is responsible for the initial capture of ICH elements using high-resolution 3D scanning technologies and advanced photography. The precision of this layer is paramount, as it sets the stage for all subsequent digital representations.

Data Processing and Management Layer: The crux of our framework, this middleware layer employs sophisticated algorithms for data refinement, transformation, and management. It converts raw scan data into a structured format amenable to holographic rendering, with a keen focus on preserving the nuances and subtleties of the cultural artifacts.

Cloud Broadcasting Layer: Leveraging the expansive capabilities of cloud computing, this layer facilitates the real-time transmission of processed data. It ensures that the holographic content is streamed with minimal latency, allowing for global accessibility and interaction.

Presentation and Interaction Layer: The final layer in our architecture, it is where the digital content is rendered and displayed using state-of-the-art holographic projection systems. This layer also incorporates interactive components, allowing users to engage with the ICH in an immersive and intuitive manner.

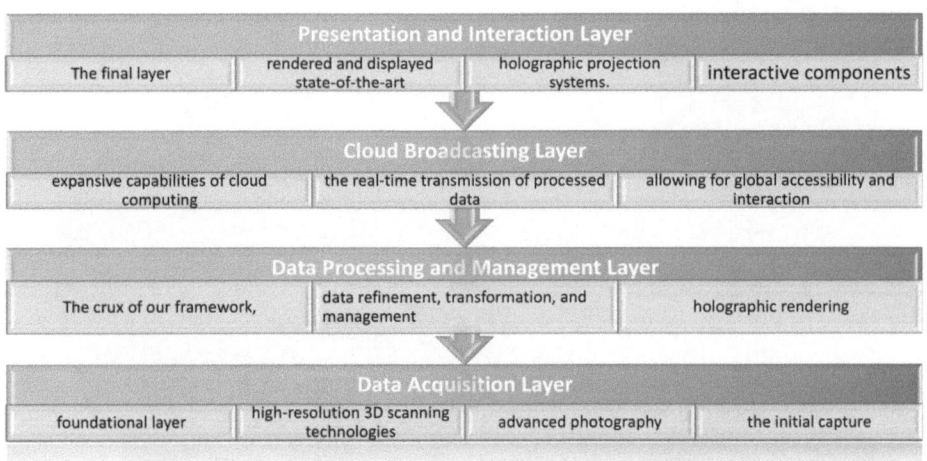

Fig. 1. System Architecture

3.2 Technological Constructs

Our framework is underpinned by cutting-edge technologies, each chosen for its ability to contribute to the seamless preservation and exhibition of ICH:

$$I(x, y) = |E(x, y)|^2 = |O + R|^2 \tag{1}$$

Holographic Technology: We harness the potential of digital holography to create three-dimensional representations that are not merely visually accurate but also culturally resonant.

Cloud Computing: By utilizing cloud infrastructure, we ensure that our system is scalable, reliable, and capable of handling the vast amounts of data generated during the digitization process.

Advancements in Display: The latest in display technology are employed to deliver high-fidelity holographic projections that bring the ICH to life, providing an experience that is both educational and emotionally impactful.

3.3 Data Acquisition and Digital Conversion

The process of data acquisition is executed with a combination of 3D laser scanning and photogrammetry, ensuring that the digital twins of ICH elements are created with micron-level accuracy. Post-capture, the data undergoes a meticulous digital conversion process, where it is cleaned, aligned, and optimized for the holographic display (Fig. 2).

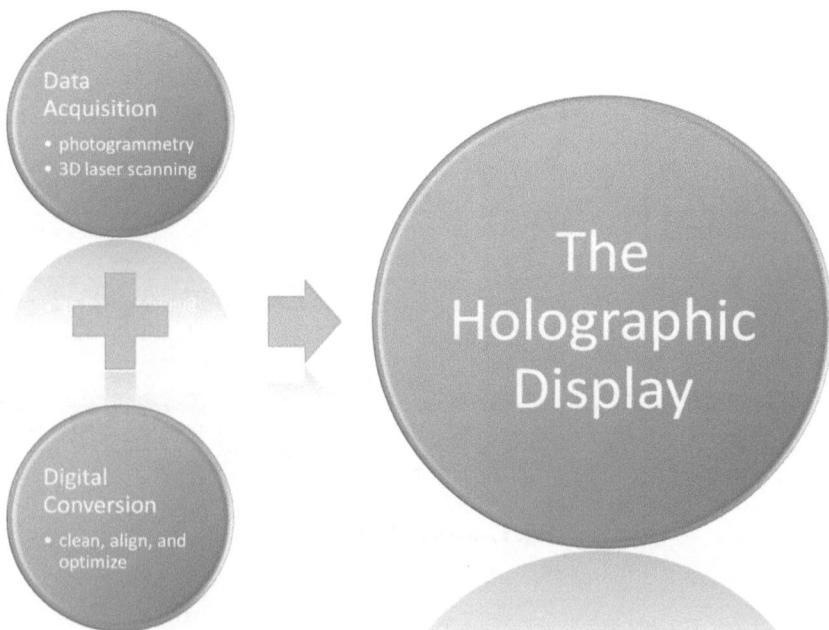

Fig. 2. Data Acquisition and Digital Conversion

3.4   Real-Time Cloud Broadcasting System

The broadcasting system is designed with a focus on efficiency and reliability. By employing advanced network protocols and leveraging the distributed nature of cloud computing, we achieve a balance between high data throughput and minimal transmission delays. This system ensures that the holographic content is delivered in real-time, providing a consistent and engaging user experience regardless of geographical location (Fig. 3).

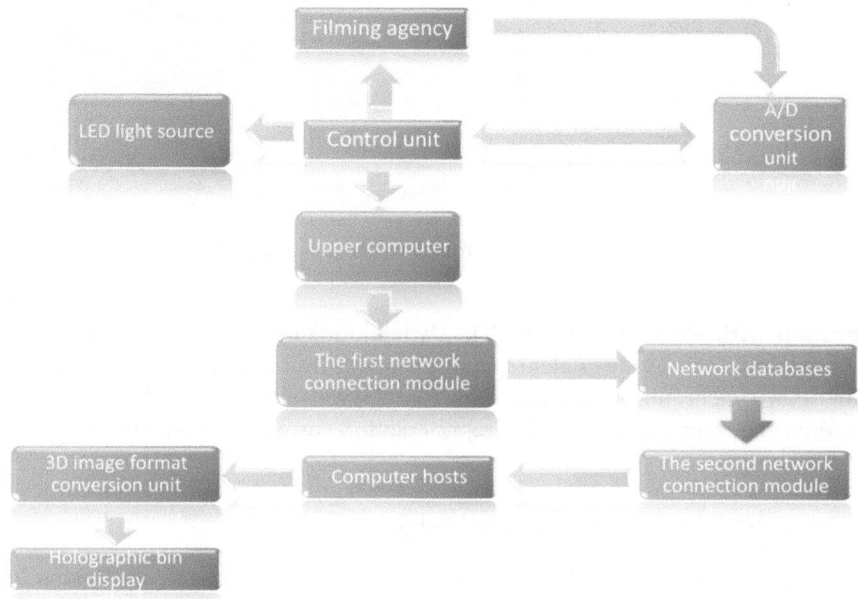

Fig. 3. Real-time Cloud Broadcasting System

As we progress through the subsequent sections, we will explore each layer and technological component in greater depth, elucidating the mechanisms that drive our framework and the innovative solutions we have developed to address the unique challenges posed by the digital preservation of intangible cultural heritage.

3.5   Holographic Projection and Display System

The holographic projection and display system stands as a testament to technological prowess, meticulously designed to bring the intangible to life (Fig. 4).

Technical Specifications: Our system is equipped with high-resolution lasers and light-field displays that facilitate crisp, clear holographic images with exceptional depth cues. The choice of coherent light sources and modulators ensures that the system can reproduce the subtlest of details, critical for cultural authenticity.

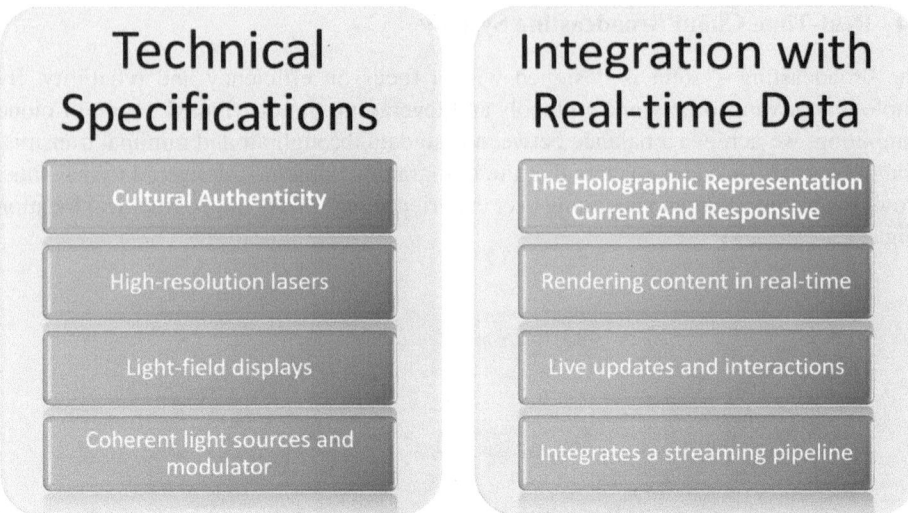

Fig. 4. Holographic Projection and Display System

Integration with Real-Time Data: The dynamic nature of ICH demands a display system capable of rendering content in real-time. Our framework integrates a streaming pipeline that synchronizes data from the cloud layer, allowing for live updates and interactions that keep the holographic representation current and responsive.

3.6   User Interaction and Experience Design

The engagement of users with holographic content is paramount, and our **Design Principles** are centered around creating an inclusive and intuitive experience. We employ user-centered design methodologies to craft interfaces that are accessible to a diverse audience, from ICH experts to the general public.

Interactive Elements: The system features touch-based and gesture-recognition technologies that allow users to navigate through the holographic space, explore cultural artifacts from various angles, and delve into informational layers associated with the heritage elements.

Feedback Mechanisms: Immediate and informative feedback is provided to users to enhance interaction. Haptic, auditory, and visual cues are integrated to offer a multi-sensory experience, enriching the user's connection with the ICH.

3.7   System Integration and Interoperability

The seamless operation of our framework relies on the harmonious integration of its subsystems.

Strategies for Integration: We adopt a middleware approach that acts as an intermediary, managing the communication between the data acquisition, processing, cloud broadcasting, and display layers. This ensures a cohesive workflow and data integrity throughout the system.

Ensuring Compatibility: Adhering to industry standards and open protocols ensures that our system is compatible with a range of devices and software platforms. This interoperability allows for the integration of additional tools and services as the field evolves.

3.8 Technical Challenges and Solutions

The path to technological innovation is often fraught with challenges.

Identification of Technical Hurdles: Key among these are data security in the cloud, the bandwidth required for real-time holographic rendering, and the preservation of cultural context in an interactive environment.

Innovative Solutions: To address these, we implement end-to-end encryption for data security, leverage adaptive bitrate streaming to manage bandwidth variability, and develop context-aware algorithms that enrich the user's interactive experience without compromising cultural integrity.

4 Case Study in ICH Protection Application

4.1 Application of the Framework

The application of our technological framework in the preservation of ICH is grounded in a profound respect for cultural diversity and a commitment to ensuring the longevity of cultural practices. The framework is designed to be adaptable to various forms of ICH, from traditional crafts to performing arts, offering a flexible yet comprehensive solution for digitization and presentation (Fig. 5).

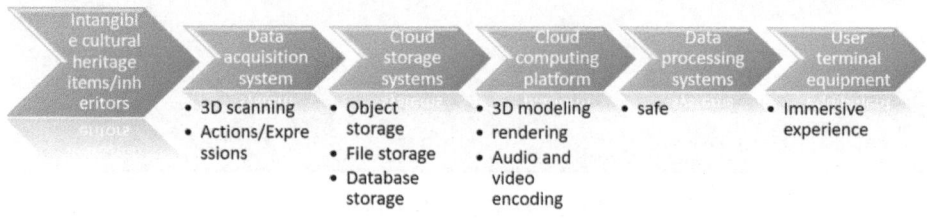

Fig. 5. Application of the Framework

Digitization Process: The framework is applied by first conducting a thorough assessment of the ICH element to be preserved. This includes detailed documentation and the selection of appropriate capture techniques that best represent the unique characteristics of the heritage. The digitization process is then executed with the utmost precision, utilizing the advanced data acquisition and processing methods outlined in our framework.

Preservation and Accessibility: Once digitized, the ICH elements are stored in a secure cloud environment, ensuring their preservation for future generations. The framework also facilitates easy access and sharing, allowing cultural institutions and the public to engage with the ICH in a meaningful way.

4.2   Case Study: Digital Exhibition of Traditional Crafts

A case study demonstrating the application of our framework is the digital exhibition of traditional crafts. This project involved the digitization of intricate textile patterns and the creation of a virtual loom, allowing users to interact with the craft and learn about the techniques and cultural significance.

Image 1. Digital Exhibition

Implementation: High-resolution 3D scanning was employed to capture the texture and design of the textiles. The data was then processed and rendered into holographic models, which were integrated into a virtual exhibition space. Users could explore the exhibition through a web-based interface, providing an accessible platform for a global audience.

Outcomes: The digital exhibition not only served as a preservation tool but also as an educational resource. It allowed viewers to understand the complexity of the craft and appreciate the cultural heritage in a modern context. The interactive elements of the exhibition, such as the virtual loom, provided a hands-on experience that was both engaging and informative.

4.3 Case Study: Virtual Performance of Traditional Music

Another application of our framework is in the virtual performance of traditional music, where the challenge lies in capturing the acoustic properties and the cultural context of the performance.

Image 2. Virtual Performance of Traditional Music

Implementation: Utilizing advanced audio capture techniques, we recorded the music with a focus on preserving the nuances of the performance. The audio data was then synchronized with holographic images of the musicians, creating a lifelike representation of the traditional performance.

Outcomes: The virtual performance was showcased in a dedicated space, where visitors could experience the music in an immersive environment. The framework's user interaction design allowed for a deeper exploration of the music, including the history of the instruments and the cultural context of the performance.

The application of our framework in ICH protection has demonstrated its effectiveness in preserving and presenting cultural heritage in a digital format. The case studies highlight the framework's ability to adapt to different forms of ICH and provide engaging experiences for users. As technology continues to evolve, so too will our framework, ensuring that the rich tapestry of intangible cultural heritage is preserved and appreciated for generations to come.

5   Discussion and Prospects

5.1   Summary of Achievements

The integration of our technological framework into the domain of intangible cultural heritage (ICH) has yielded significant achievements. It has successfully digitized various forms of ICH, providing innovative methods for preservation, access, and interaction. The framework's adaptability has been particularly noteworthy, catering to the unique challenges posed by different cultural elements.

5.2   Challenges and Solutions

While our framework has demonstrated success, challenges remain, particularly in the areas of:

Data Security: Ensuring the secure storage and transmission of digitized ICH data, safeguarding against unauthorized access and potential data breaches.

Cultural Misinterpretation: Avoiding misinterpretation and ensuring that the digital representations of ICH are contextually accurate and respectful.

Resource Allocation: Balancing the allocation of resources to both the technological development and the cultural engagement aspects of the framework.

5.3   Future Directions

As we reflect on the current state of our framework, several future directions present themselves, offering opportunities for enhancement and expansion:

Technological Advancements: With the rapid evolution of technology, especially in the fields of artificial intelligence and virtual reality, there is potential to further refine the user experience and automate preservation processes.

Cultural Relevance: Ensuring that our framework remains culturally relevant is crucial. This involves continuous engagement with cultural communities to accurately represent their heritage.

Scalability and Sustainability: Addressing the scalability of the framework to accommodate a growing number of ICH elements and ensuring the long-term sustainability of digital preservation efforts.

Educational Outreach: Leveraging the framework as an educational tool to increase awareness and understanding of ICH among younger generations.

Policy and Ethical Frameworks: Developing robust policy and ethical guidelines that govern the use and dissemination of digitized ICH to protect cultural integrity and intellectual property rights.

In conclusion, the journey of integrating technology with the preservation of intangible cultural heritage is both a scientific endeavor and a cultural responsibility. As we look to the future, it is with a commitment to continuous improvement, ethical stewardship, and a deep respect for the rich tapestry of human culture that we carry forward our work.

Acknowledgements. This research has received substantial support from: 1. Research on Legal Protection of Big Data Trading Security in Hubei Province, funding reference number: 19ZD077. 2. Research Project of Hubei Provincial China Vocational Education Association in 2024, funding reference number: MJH24578-8.

Funding. This research was funded by Research on Engineering Cognition and Innovation Capability Cultivation for Freshmen in the Context of New Engineering Education at Colleges and Universities., funding reference number: 2019GA066.

Conflicts of Interest. The authors declare no conflicts of interest.

References

1. Yang, J., Xu, C.: Digital enabling rural revitalization: an innovative study of intangible cultural heritage in animation-based inheritance and dissemination. Appl. Math. Nonlinear Sci. **9**(1) (2024). https://doi.org/10.2478/amns-2024-1674
2. Xia, H., Li, Y., Chen, F., et al.: The influence of participant subject factors on collaboration effects in the protection of China's ICH: the mediating role of relationship quality. Sustainability **14** (2022). https://doi.org/10.3390/su14031223
3. Yaan, M.Y., Keir, S., Hkelek, B., et al.: Multi-user directional modulation with reconfigurable holographic surfaces. EURASIP J. Wirel. Commun. Netw. **2024**(1) (2024). https://doi.org/10.1186/s13638-024-02383-3
4. Kim, Y.: Sup. assessment of legality of local government regulations - including assessment of problems in "cultural heritage protection regulations of Seoul special metropolitan city. Adm. Law J. (44), 99–128 (2016)
5. Tang, T., Zhang, H.: An Interactive Holographic Multimedia Technology and Its Application in the Preservation and Dissemination of Intangible Cultural Heritage (2023)
6. Sugie, T., Akamatsu, T., Nishitsuji, T., et al.: High-performance parallel computing for next-generation holographic imaging. Nat. Electron. **1**, 254–259 (2018)
7. Bilis, T., Kouimtzoglou, T., Magnisali, M., et al.: The use of 3D scanning and photogrammetry techniques in the case study of the roman theatre of Nikopolis. Surveying, virtual reconstruction and restoration study. ISPRS Int. Arch. Photogram. Remote Sens. Spatial Inf. Sci. XLII-2/W3, 97–103 (2017). https://doi.org/10.5194/isprs-archives-XLII-2-W3-97-2017
8. Park, H.J., Lee, B.: Holographic techniques for augmented reality and virtual reality near-eye displays. Light Adv. Manufact. **3**(1), 137–150 (2022)

9. Mendoza, M.A.D., De La Hoz Franco, E.., Gómez, J.E.G.: Technologies for the preservation of cultural heritage—a systematic review of the literature. Sustainbility **15**(2), 1059 (2023)
10. Adam, S.: Preserving authenticity in the digital age. Library hi tech **28**(4), 595–604 (2010)
11. Chen, S.: Analysis of the ecological protection and inheritance path of intangible cultural heritage enabled by digital technology—take the national intangible cultural heritage "Cuo Taiji" as an example. J. Sociol. Ethnol. **5**(10) (2023)

Node Pressure Prediction by Aggregating Long-Range Information

Pinghua Xu[1,2], Wenhang Yu[3,4], Xu Zhou[1], Xiaofan Chen[1(✉)],
and Kejiang Ye[2(✉)]

[1] Sangfor Technologies Inc., Shenzhen, China
`xupinghua@whu.edu.cn`, {`zhouxu,chenxiaofan`}`@sangfor.com.cn`
[2] Shenzhen Institute of Advanced Technology, Chinese Academy of Sciences,
Shenzhen, China
`kj.ye@siat.ac.cn`
[3] Changjiang Schinta Software Technology Co. LTD., Wuhan, China
`haldate@whu.edu.cn`
[4] Internet+ Intelligent Water Conservancy Key Laboratory of Changjiang Water
Resources Commission, Wuhan, China

Abstract. Predicting node pressure accurately is of paramount importance for the management of water distribution networks (WDNs). Recent advances have highlighted the efficacy of graph neural networks (GNNs), tailored for data with inherent graph structures, in addressing this challenge. However, the performance of extant GNN-based approaches is constrained by their limited capacity to harness long-range dependencies within the network. To address this limitation, we introduce a novel long-range adaptive convolution network. Inspired by the graph kernel, our method possesses a broad receptive field, while the flexibility of information aggregation is enhanced through the attention mechanism. Additionally, we incorporate residuals specifically engineered for WDN applications to further refine our prediction accuracy. Our comprehensive evaluations on three real-world WDN datasets reveal that our method consistently surpasses existing benchmarks. We have made the code and experimental datasets publicly accessible via a GitHub repository (https://github.com/Haldate-Yu/GAL-WDN).

Keywords: Graph neural network · Water distribution network · Node pressure prediction

1 Introduction

Water distribution networks (WDNs) facilitate the conveyance of treated water from treatment plants to consumers across residential, commercial, and industrial sectors. Predicting node pressure is essential for estimating the hydraulic pressure at various junction points within a WDN. This prediction is crucial for the effective management and operation of WDNs, ensuring the provision of a

© The Author(s), under exclusive license to Springer Nature Switzerland AG 2025
S. Zhang and L.-J. Zhang (Eds.): SCF 2024 - ICIOT 2024, LNCS 15427, pp. 53–65, 2025.
https://doi.org/10.1007/978-3-031-77003-6_5

dependable and efficient water supply to all users. Moreover, accurate node pressure prediction is instrumental in maintaining and safety, as well as in mitigating the risk of leaks and bursts.

Accurately predicting node pressure within WDNs is an essential yet challenging task. The principal challenge arises from data scarcity, as cost constraints typically mean that only a subset of nodes within a network are equipped with sensors, impeding the ability to fully ascertain the system's condition. This limitation obstructs the effective simulation and computation of network behavior through physics-based models, which rely on fluid mechanics principles. Additionally, these models demand considerable expertise for precise configuration and interpretation of outcomes [4,10]. Their complexity renders them non-transferable across systems with varying network configurations and operational conditions.

Building on the aforementioned challenges inherent in WDNs, graph neural networks (GNNs) have surfaced as a useful tool, markedly enhancing our analytical capabilities within this sphere. GNNs are especially adept at navigating the intricate, interwoven architecture of WDNs [2,17] because conceptualizing a WDN as a graph naturally aligns with their structure, where nodes represent junctions and edges represent the conduits or pathways of flow between these junctions. As data-driven constructs, GNNs have the potential to utilize extant partial data to extrapolate the conditions of unmonitored segments of the network. Although GNN-based methods have outperformed traditional approaches, they are not without their constraints. In WDNs, the pressure at various nodes is highly interdependent, and the pressure readings available for observation are exceedingly sparse. This scarcity necessitates the incorporation of long-range data to yield accurate predictions. Despite this imperative, contemporary methods fall short in effectively harnessing such long-range information, thereby leading to suboptimal performance.

To address this research void, we propose a graph attention network with a long-range receptive field (GAL), designed to capture long-range dependencies effectively and flexibly. Prevailing methodologies, such as GDC [9] and SSGC [21], have demonstrated that kernel functions are effective in extending the receptive field. However, they typically employ a limited number of layers—commonly a single layer—to circumvent the issue of over-smoothing, which can impair the fitting capabilities of neural networks. WDNs, characterized by their inherent sparsity, are less prone to over-smoothing resulting from multiple layers. Consequently, we have extended SSGC to develop a rudimentary version of GAL, which is capable of learning more expressive representations at each layer. We have retained the feature of layer-level aggregation, which is instrumental in generating high-quality representations. To enhance the flexibility of message propagation, we have integrated an attention mechanism into each convolutional layer. Given the significance of the initial node feature in WDNs, we incorporate this feature as a residual component within our methodology to refine the representations learned. In summary, our principal contributions are delineated as follows.

- We have developed an innovative graph neural network model for predicting node pressure within WDNs, which is capable of effectively capturing long-range information.
- We conducted a comprehensive series of experiments utilizing multiple real-world datasets to substantiate the superior performance of our proposed method over existing state-of-the-art GNN approaches in the task of node pressure prediction.
- All methodologies and experimental data generation processes have been fully integrated into a dedicated code repository. This integration facilitates the reproducibility of the reported results, enabling researchers to efficiently build upon our work.

The remainder of this paper is structured as follows: Sect. 2 delineates the background and context of the study. Section 3 describes our methodology in detail. Section 4 presents the experiments and includes a comprehensive discussion of the results. Finally, Sect. 5 concludes the paper and outlines implications and potential avenues for future research.

2   Background

2.1   Related Works

Graph Neural Networks. Graph Neural Networks (GNNs) have emerged as a powerful class of neural networks adept at handling data with inherent graph structures, as originally outlined by Veličković et al. [14]. Predominantly, GNNs operate on the principle of message passing, wherein nodes dynamically assimilate information from their immediate surroundings using differentiable aggregation and combination operations. This process is typically confined to a localized neighborhood, commonly referred to as the low-hop vicinity, where each node integrates messages from its neighbors. Subsequently, these aggregated inputs are merged with the node's previous representation. In recent years, the application of GNNs has been extended to specialized fields, including remote sensing [6] and biological systems [22]. Despite these advancements, the potential of GNNs within the context of WDNs remains largely uncharted territory.

GNNs in WDNs. Pressure estimation is essential for the management, monitoring, and maintenance of WDNs, facilitating leak detection and optimal control. Recent studies have applied Graph Neural Networks (GNNs) to this task, with notable progress [1,5,13]. Spectral GCNs, introduced in [1], showed initial success, but their reliance on local graph structure limited performance. Spatial GCNs, as proposed in [5], and attention mechanisms, as implemented in [13], have since improved accuracy. Despite these advances, existing GNN methods face challenges in leveraging long-range dependencies for precise predictions. To overcome this, we propose a novel approach that excels at capturing long-range information, delivering impressive results in our experiments.

2.2   Preliminaries

Notation. We follow the matrix cookbook [11] to formulate notations used in this paper. Let $\mathcal{G} = (\mathcal{V}, \mathcal{E}, \mathbf{y})$ be a WDN, where $\mathcal{V}$ is the node set representing junctions, $\mathcal{E}$ is the edge set representing pipes, $\mathbf{y}$ is the node pressure values, and N will refer to the cardinality of $\mathcal{V}$. The i-th element y_i of $\mathbf{y}$ represents the i-th node's pressure. In the real world, $\mathbf{y}$ is usually partially observable because only a subset of nodes have sensors. We denote $\mathbf{x}$ as the observable pressure values and utilize zero to impute missing values. We use $\mathbf{A} \in \{0,1\}^{N \times N}$ to describe the network topology, where $A_{ij} = 1$ indicates an edge between the i-th node and j-th node, and $A_{ij} = 0$ indicates that the i-th node and j-th node are not connected. Let $\mathbf{D}$ be the row connectivity matrix, where $D_{ii} = \sum_{j=1}^{N} |A_{ij}|$ and all the other entries are zeros. We then have the transition probability matrix $\mathbf{P} = \mathbf{D}^{-1}\mathbf{A}$.

Problem Formulation. The objective of node pressure prediction is to estimate the unobserved pressure values within a network using the available pressure data and the underlying network topology. Formally, this task can be articulated as follows:

$$\min L(M(\mathbf{A}, \mathbf{x}), \mathbf{y}), \tag{1}$$

where L represents the loss function that quantifies the discrepancy between the predicted and actual signals and M denotes the predictive model. Given that node pressure values fluctuate temporally, the network can be segmented into discrete temporal slices, or snapshots. Typically, model M is calibrated on preceding snapshots and subsequently employed to forecast future snapshots. The predictive accuracy of the model is commonly assessed by averaging the results across these subsequent snapshots to determine the overall performance.

3   Methodology

3.1   Our Method

In water distribution networks, the pressure at any given node is influenced by the conditions of adjacent nodes. This interconnectedness arises from several factors: 1. Water, as it flows through the network, incurs head losses due to friction and encounters a variety of impediments, which affect the downstream pressure. 2. Variations in water consumption can induce pressure fluctuations; an increase in demand at one node can reduce the pressure at that point, potentially impacting neighboring nodes as well. 3. Operational modifications, such as the adjustment of pumps or valves, can precipitate immediate and extensive alterations in pressure throughout the network. Recognizing the interdependence of nodal pressures is crucial for accurate pressure prediction at a specific node. However, the pressures at most nodes are not directly observable due to financial limitations; sensors are typically installed on only a select few nodes. Moreover, many nodes are incapable of collecting meaningful data if their receptive field is

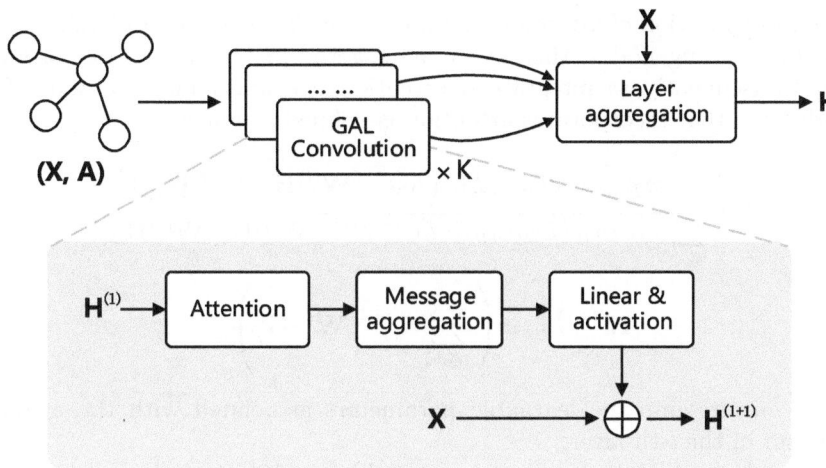

Fig. 1. Architecture of the proposed GAL model.

overly restricted. Consequently, enhancing the receptive field of GNNs is essential for achieving improved predictive performance.

Kernel-based GNNs offer significant benefits in expanding the receptive field, with the Simplified Spectral Graph Convolution (SSGC) model being particularly noteworthy. The formulation of SSGC is presented as follows:

$$\frac{1}{L}\sum_{l=1}^{L}\mathbf{T}^l\mathbf{X}\mathbf{W}, \tag{2}$$

where $\mathbf{T}$ is the transition matrix derived from $\mathbf{A}$. The SSGC model leverages the Markov diffusion kernel [3] to expand its receptive field. Typically, SSGC employs a singular nonlinear transformation.

The addition of multiple nonlinear layers is hypothesized to enhance the model's fitting capabilities; however, this strategy is also a primary contributor to the phenomenon of over-smoothing [7]. Consequently, GNNs typically incorporate fewer than four nonlinear layers. In contrast, WDNs, which are the subject of less frequent academic inquiry, exhibit a high degree of sparsity and are less susceptible to over-smoothing. This characteristic allows for the integration of nonlinear transformations into each layer to bolster the model's fitting capacity:

$$\mathbf{H}^{(l+1)} = \sigma(\mathbf{T}\mathbf{X}\mathbf{W}^{(l)}), \tag{3}$$

where $\mathbf{H}^{(l)}$ denotes the representations of l-th layer and σ denotes the activation function. We follow SSGC to adopt the layer-level feature aggregation to refine the final node representations:

$$\mathbf{H} = \frac{1}{L}\sum_{l=1}^{L}\mathbf{H}^{(l)}. \tag{4}$$

The incorporation of attention mechanisms facilitates more tailored message aggregation among nodes, thereby enhancing the fitting capabilities of GNNs [15,20]. Consequently, we integrate an attention mechanism into our model. Each network layer that incorporates attention is defined as follows:

$$\alpha_{ij}^{(l)} = \frac{exp\left(LeackyReLU\left(\mathbf{a}^{(l)^\top}\left[\mathbf{W}^{(l)}\mathbf{H}_i||\mathbf{W}^{(l)}\mathbf{H}_j\right]\right)\right)}{\sum_{k\in\mathcal{N}_i} exp\left(LeackyReLU\left(\mathbf{a}^{(l)^\top}\left[\mathbf{W}^{(l)}\mathbf{H}_i||\mathbf{W}^{(l)}\mathbf{H}_k\right]\right)\right)}, \tag{5}$$

$$\mathbf{H}^{(l+1)} = \sigma\left(\sum_{j\in\mathcal{N}_i}\alpha_{ij}^{(l+1)}\mathbf{W}^{(l)}\mathbf{H}_j^l\right), \tag{6}$$

where $\mathbf{a}^{(l)}$ represents the learnable parameters associated with the attention mechanism in the l-th layer.

In accordance with the findings presented in [18,19], the initial node features are crucial for node prediction tasks, as they encapsulate the distinctive information pertinent to each node. To enhance the exploitation of this information, we incorporate $\mathbf{X}$ into each aggregation layer in the form of a residual connection:

$$\mathbf{H}^{(l+1)} = \sigma\left(\sum_{j\in\mathcal{N}_i}\alpha_{ij}^{(l+1)}\mathbf{W}^{(l)}\mathbf{H}_j^l + \beta\mathbf{X}\right), \tag{7}$$

$$\mathbf{H} = \frac{1}{L}\sum_{l=1}^{L}\mathbf{H}^{(l)} + \beta\mathbf{X}, \tag{8}$$

where β represents the significance attributed to the initial features. While the magnitude of this parameter is not the central concern of our investigation, for the purposes of consistency and simplicity, we have elected to set β equal to 1 for all subsequent analyses presented herein.

In conclusion, we have developed a graph neural network for WDNs that captures long-range dependencies and exhibits a robust fitting capability. Drawing inspiration from kernel-based methodologies, we initially establish a foundational version of our approach, as delineated in Eqs. (3) and (4). Subsequently, we integrate an attention mechanism to enhance the model's fitting capability, as detailed in Eqs. (5) and (6). Finally, we incorporate initial features as residuals to further refine the quality of the representations, as indicated in Eqs. (7) and (8). Figure 1 illustrates the network architecture of our GAL method. The efficacy of this progressively structured design is evidenced in the ablation study presented in Sect. 4.3.

3.2   Discussion

Relation of GAL to SSGC. In Eq. (2), SSGC facilitates long-range message aggregation via Markov diffusion kernels. While our approach draws inspiration from SSGC, we incorporate a non-linear mapping at each stage of aggregation to enhance the model's fitting capability. Furthermore, we substitute the transition-based message aggregation mechanism with an attention-based approach. Consequently, the network architecture of the GAL diverges significantly from that of SSGC.

Relation of GAL to GAT. GAT [14] pioneered the incorporation of the attention mechanism within GNNs. Inspired by GAT, our GAL method similarly employs the attention mechanism. Nevertheless, GAT differs from GAL in that it does not implement layer-level feature aggregation or utilize an initial feature residual. These distinctions contribute to the unique characteristics of GAL in comparison to its predecessor.

Relation of GAL to GATRes. GATRes [13] represents a specialized variant of GAT tailored for WDNs. GATRes introduces an auxiliary attention layer to appraise head views emanating from its antecedent layer, thereby establishing a distinct message aggregation mechanism. Additionally, our GAL method diverges from GATRes by residual and layer-level feature aggregation.

4   Experiments

In this section, we present a comprehensive series of experiments designed to assess the efficacy of our proposed method. Specifically, we address the following research questions (RQs):

- **RQ1**: Does the GAL approach outperform the classical GNN methods? (see Sect. 4.2)
- **RQ2**: Does the GAL approach exhibit competitive performance in comparison to GNN methodologies expressly tailored for WDNs? (see Sect. 4.2)
- **RQ3**: How the layer stacking, the integration of attention mechanisms, and the implementation of initial feature residuals enhance model performance? (see Sect. 4.3)

4.1   Experimental Setup

Datasets. In this research, we employed three WDNs: the fictional Anytown and C-Town, and the real-world Richmond, which boasts a population of approximately 8,000 inhabitants. Our approach to sensor placement was informed by the strategies delineated in [5]. A comprehensive statistical overview of these networks is encapsulated in Table 1. We embraced the dataset generation techniques pioneered by [5], capturing a sequence of 1,000 consecutive time steps for each network. To emulate the deployment of sensors within the WDNs, we crafted a binary mask that corresponds to the node count, as meticulously outlined in [1]. For each network, we explored three levels of sensor sparsity: 0.05, 0.1, and 0.2.

Table 1. Water distribution network statistics.

WDN	# Nodes	# Edges	Diameter	Average degree
Anytown	22	41	5	3.60
C-Town	388	429	66	2.24
Richmond	865	949	234	2.19

The decision to forgo the examination of higher sparsity levels was driven by their diminished complexity. For each sparsity level and WDS, we produced five unique random sensor configurations. The simulations were conducted utilizing the EPANET toolkit, as referenced in [12].

Comparative Methods. To address RQ1, we selected classic GNN methods for comparison, including GCN [8], SGC [16], and SSGC [21]. Additionally, to address RQ2, we have selected GNN methodologies specifically designed for WDN for comparison, including GraphConWat [1], mGCN [5], and GATRes [13].

Parameter Setting. For the spectral GCN baseline, GraphConvWat, which employs a K-localized spectral filter, we selected a learning rate of 3e−4 and a weight decay of 1e−6. Our other model settings closely mirror those established in [1]. Moving on to the spatial GCN baseline, mGCN, which capitalizes on edge features, we set the learning rate to 5e−4 and omitted weight decay. For additional parameters such as the number of hops, MLP layers, and the latent dimension, we adhered to the configurations delineated in [5]. For the attention-based GNN baseline, GATRes, which is distinguished by its reliance on an attention mechanism, we adopted the hyperparameters specified in [13]. Specifically, we applied a learning rate of 5e−4 and a weight decay of 1e−6 for both the GATRes-Small and GATRes-Large models. Our proposed method, GAL, was configured with a learning rate of 5e−4 and a weight decay of 1e−6. The number of layers was tailored to the specific WDN, with 8 layers for Anytown and 32 layers for both C-Town and Richmond. Additionally, we set the hidden size to 128 for Anytown and 256 for C-Town and Richmond. All models were implemented within the PyTorch framework, utilizing the Adam optimizer and subjected to training over 2,000 epochs. We incorporated an early stopping criterion that terminates training after 250 epochs if the loss variation is less than 1e−6, thereby preventing overfitting and enhancing computational efficiency.

Evaluation. We follow [1] and [5] to use the mean relative absolute error for evaluation. The metric is defined as follows:

$$Error = \frac{1}{S \cdot N} \sum_{i=1}^{S} \sum_{v=1}^{N} \frac{|y_{iv} - \hat{y_{iv}}|}{y_{iv}}, \tag{9}$$

where y_{iv} represents the ground truth and S represents the number of samples in a mini-batch.

Table 2. Experimental results on the Anytown dataset.

Type	Method	$\alpha = 0.05$	$\alpha = 0.1$	$\alpha = 0.2$
Classical GNN	GCN	0.168 ± 0.157	0.163 ± 0.161	0.161 ± 0.162
	SGC	0.817 ± 0.022	0.882 ± 0.060	0.885 ± 0.091
	SSGC	0.828 ± 0.019	0.801 ± 0.044	0.816 ± 0.045
GNN for WDN	GATRes-small	0.164 ± 0.161	0.164 ± 0.162	0.153 ± 0.167
	GATRes-large	0.189 ± 0.155	0.176 ± 0.160	0.167 ± 0.164
	mGCN	3.080 ± 4.604	3.107 ± 4.712	3.215 ± 4.959
	GraphConvWat	0.181 ± 0.162	0.174 ± 0.175	0.329 ± 0.376
Ours	GAL	$\mathbf{0.155} \pm 0.161$	$\mathbf{0.154} \pm 0.161$	$\mathbf{0.145} \pm 0.166$

Table 3. Experimental results on the Ctown dataset.

Type	Method	$\alpha = 0.05$	$\alpha = 0.1$	$\alpha = 0.2$
Classical GNN	GCN	0.801 ± 0.251	0.758 ± 0.227	0.588 ± 0.240
	SGC	1.891 ± 0.211	1.763 ± 0.311	1.618 ± 0.309
	SSGC	1.854 ± 0.253	1.794 ± 0.311	1.607 ± 0.342
GNN for WDN	GATRes-small	0.125 ± 0.032	0.123 ± 0.035	0.119 ± 0.027
	GATRes-large	$\mathbf{0.113} \pm 0.040$	0.119 ± 0.058	0.118 ± 0.045
	mGCN	0.716 ± 0.116	0.724 ± 0.122	0.740 ± 0.133
	GraphConvWat	0.483 ± 0.214	0.576 ± 0.275	0.739 ± 0.344
Ours	GAL	0.120 ± 0.040	$\mathbf{0.095} \pm 0.030$	$\mathbf{0.096} \pm 0.043$

4.2   Results (for RQ1 and RQ2)

The results delineated in Tables 2, 3 and 4 offer a comprehensive comparison of various GNNs as applied to the datasets from Anytown, Ctown, and Richmond.

Classical GNN models, specifically SGC and SSGC, manifest a progressive deterioration in performance with increasing values of α. This trend underscores the enhanced predictive accuracy achievable with greater volumes of observable data. Within the classical GNN paradigm, SGC demonstrates a marginal superiority over SSGC at $\alpha = 0.05$ in Richmond, hinting at a potential benefit in precision. Conversely, in Ctown, SSGC outperforms SGC slightly at all α levels, revealing an interaction that is contingent on the specific dataset. The GATRes-small and GATRes-large models show a consistent performance pattern, with negligible differences between them, suggesting that the larger model does not inherently provide superior results. This observation may be ascribed to the particular attributes of the datasets or the intrinsic efficiency of the models' architectures. GraphConvWat reveals a marked decrement in efficacy when α escalates from 0.1 to 0.2 in the Ctown dataset, a pattern absent in the other datasets. This could suggest that GraphConvWat is particularly attuned to specific characteristics of the Ctown data. Finally, the proposed GAL model surpasses all

Table 4. Experimental results on the Richmond dataset.

Type	Method	$\alpha = 0.05$	$\alpha = 0.1$	$\alpha = 0.2$
Classical GNN	GCN	0.578 ± 0.238	0.505 ± 0.291	0.376 ± 0.311
	SGC	0.792 ± 0.190	0.689 ± 0.235	0.629 ± 0.267
	SSGC	0.814 ± 0.193	0.713 ± 0.244	0.626 ± 0.288
GNN for WDN	GATRes-small	0.124 ± 0.070	0.122 ± 0.140	0.099 ± 0.125
	GATRes-large	0.181 ± 0.210	0.177 ± 0.214	0.150 ± 0.206
	mGCN	0.131 ± 0.011	0.133 ± 0.013	0.138 ± 0.017
	GraphConvWat	0.207 ± 0.098	0.211 ± 0.074	0.219 ± 0.067
Ours	GAL	$\mathbf{0.102} \pm 0.095$	$\mathbf{0.079} \pm 0.091$	$\mathbf{0.093} \pm 0.145$

competing models in nearly every dataset and across all α levels, indicating that GAL has a robust and versatile architecture that generalizes effectively across varied datasets and significance thresholds.

In conclusion, the proposed GAL model exhibits consistently superior performance, indicating that it integrates mechanisms advantageous for a diverse array of graph-based tasks. GAL's robustness, especially relative to competing models, renders it a compelling subject for continued investigation and potential integration within the domain of GNN research. Moreover, the findings underscore the imperative for GNN models to demonstrate adaptability and resilience across various datasets and thresholds, a requirement essential for their practical deployment.

4.3   Ablation Study (for RQ3)

Figure 2 presents a comprehensive ablation study conducted across the datasets of Anytown, Ctown, and Richmond. The initial SSGC model establishes a benchmark for subsequent comparisons. It is noted that with the increment of the hyperparameter α, SSGC's performance exhibits an improvement, aligning with the anticipated notion that an increase in training data typically fosters better generalization in models. Nevertheless, the enhancements are slight, implying that SSGC may not be optimizing the use of the data at its disposal. In contrast, the second method, GAL w/o. attn & residual, integrates a nonlinear transformation after each step of information aggregation, deviating from the linear strategy employed by SSGC. The empirical evidence indicates a marked reduction in error rates across all datasets in comparison to SSGC, underscoring the advantageous effect of this nonlinear modification. Further advancements are achieved with the introduction of GAL w/o. residual, which supplements the information aggregation framework of GAL w/o. attn & residual with an attention mechanism. This mechanism allows the model to tackle the issues such as the vanishing gradient problem and enabling the direct influence of input features on the final output.

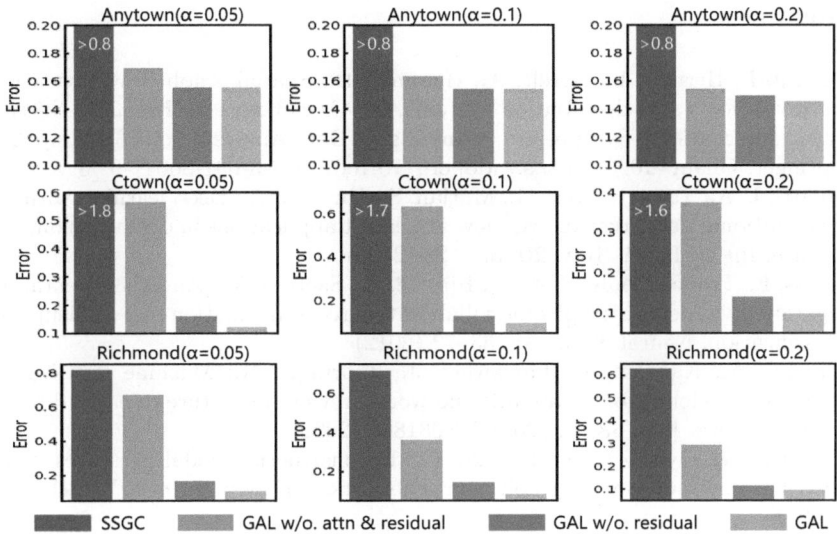

Fig. 2. Ablation study results.

A meticulous analysis of the findings delineates a consistent trajectory: each incremental addition to the model architecture yields a significant enhancement in performance. This progression from SSGC to GAL accentuates the pivotal role of sophisticated architectural design in the development of machine learning models. Nonlinear transformations, attention mechanisms, and residual connections are each pivotal in enhancing the model's learning efficacy and predictive accuracy, contributing indispensable elements to its overall performance.

5 Conclusion

In this study, we introduce an innovative graph neural network model designed to predict node pressure within WDNs. The proposed model demonstrates a marked ability to capture long-range dependencies, thereby surpassing the performance of existing methodologies. Future research will explore more versatile strategies for the integration of layer-level features, as well as the development of more efficient model architectures.

Acknowledgements. This work is supported by the National Key R&D Program of China (No. 2021YFB3300200), National Natural Science Foundation of China (No. 92267105), Guangdong Basic and Applied Basic Research Foundation (No. 2023B1515130002), Guangdong Special Support Plan (No. 2021TQ06X990), Shenzhen Basic Research Program (No. JCYJ20220818101610023, KJZD20230923113800001).

References

1. Ashraf, I., Hermes, L., Artelt, A., Hammer, B.: Spatial graph convolution neural networks for water distribution systems. In: Cremilleux, B., Hess, S., Nijssen, S. (eds.) International Symposium on Intelligent Data Analysis, vol. 13876, pp. 29–41. Springer, Cham (2023). https://doi.org/10.1007/978-3-031-30047-9_3
2. Bhatti, U.A., Tang, H., Wu, G., Marjan, S., Hussain, A.: Deep learning with graph convolutional networks: an overview and latest applications in computational intelligence. Int. J. Intell. Syst. **2023**, 1–28 (2023)
3. Fouss, F., Francoisse, K., Yen, L., Pirotte, A., Saerens, M.: An experimental investigation of kernels on graphs for collaborative recommendation and semisupervised classification. Neural Netw. **31**, 53–72 (2012)
4. Garzón, A., Kapelan, Z., Langeveld, J., Taormina, R.: Machine learning-based surrogate modeling for urban water networks: review and future research directions. Water Resour. Res. **58**(5), e2021WR031808 (2022)
5. Hajgató, G., Gyires-Tóth, B., Paál, G.: Reconstructing nodal pressures in water distribution systems with graph neural networks. arXiv preprint arXiv:2104.13619 (2021)
6. Hong, D., Gao, L., Yao, J., Zhang, B., Plaza, A., Chanussot, J.: Graph convolutional networks for hyperspectral image classification. IEEE Trans. Geosci. Remote Sens. **59**(7), 5966–5978 (2021)
7. Jin, D., et al.: Universal graph convolutional networks. In: Advances in Neural Information Processing Systems, vol. 34, pp. 10654–10664 (2021)
8. Kipf, T.N., Welling, M.: Semi-supervised classification with graph convolutional networks. In: 5th International Conference on Learning Representations (2017)
9. Klicpera, J., Weißenberger, S., Günnemann, S.: Diffusion improves graph learning. In: Advances in Neural Information Processing Systems, vol. 32, pp. 13333–13345 (2019)
10. Meirelles, G., Manzi, D., Brentan, B., Goulart, T., Luvizotto, E.: Calibration model for water distribution network using pressures estimated by artificial neural networks. Water Resour. Manage. **31**, 4339–4351 (2017)
11. Petersen, K.B., Pedersen, M.S., et al.: The matrix cookbook. Tech. Univ. Denmark **7**(15), 510 (2008)
12. Rossman, L., Woo, H., Tryby, M., Shang, F., Janke, R., Haxton, T.: EPANET 2.2 user's manual, water infrastructure division. Center for Environmental Solutions and Emergency Response (2020)
13. Truong, H., Tello, A., Lazovik, A., Degeler, V.: Graph neural networks for pressure estimation in water distribution systems. arXiv preprint arXiv:2311.10579 (2023)
14. Veličković, P., Cucurull, G., Casanova, A., Romero, A., Liò, P., Bengio, Y.: Graph attention networks. In: International Conference on Learning Representations (2018)
15. Wang, C., Tian, R., Hu, J., Ma, Z.: A trend graph attention network for traffic prediction. Inf. Sci. **623**, 275–292 (2023)
16. Wu, F., Souza, A., Zhang, T., Fifty, C., Yu, T., Weinberger, K.: Simplifying graph convolutional networks. In: International Conference on Machine Learning, pp. 6861–6871 (2019)
17. Wu, S., Sun, F., Zhang, W., Xie, X., Cui, B.: Graph neural networks in recommender systems: a survey. ACM Comput. Surv. **55**(5), 1–37 (2022)
18. Wu, Z., Jain, P., Wright, M.A., Mirhoseini, A., Gonzalez, J.E., Stoica, I.: Representing long-range context for graph neural networks with global attention. In:

Advances in Neural Information Processing Systems, vol. 34, pp. 13266–13279 (2021)

19. Yang, L., et al.: Difference residual graph neural networks. In: Proceedings of the 30th ACM International Conference on Multimedia, pp. 3356–3364 (2022)
20. Zhang, W., et al.: Graph attention multi-layer perceptron. In: Proceedings of the 28th ACM SIGKDD Conference on Knowledge Discovery and Data Mining, pp. 4560–4570 (2022)
21. Zhu, H., Koniusz, P.: Simple spectral graph convolution. In: 9th International Conference on Learning Representations (2021)
22. Zitnik, M., Agrawal, M., Leskovec, J.: Modeling polypharmacy side effects with graph convolutional networks. Bioinformatics **34**(13), i457–i466 (2018)

Novel Technology for IoT Charging Battery

Abdel-Majid Maman Guéro[1]([✉]), Noreddine Abghour[1], Zouhair Chiba[1],
Khalid Moussaid[1], Miyara Mounia[1], and Abdellah Ouaguid[2]

[1] LIS Labs, Faculty of Sciences Ain Chock, Hassan II University of Casablanca,
Casablanca, Morocco
abdelguero63@gmail.com

[2] 2IACS Laboratory, ENSET of Mohammedia, Hassan II University of Casablanca,
Casablanca, Morocco

Abstract. The Internet of Things (IoT) stands out as a dynamic and transformative force in contemporary technology, facilitating the connection of physical objects to the internet for seamless data exchange among themselves and with humans. This connectivity enables automation, real-time monitoring, and improved decision-making, fostering significant advancements across various industries and aspects of daily life. However, the proliferation of IoT devices has led to a notable surge in energy consumption, posing a considerable challenge. This paper delves into a pioneering solution aimed at mitigating the energy consumption issue inherent in the widespread adoption of IoT devices. Our approach involves tapping into the energy generated by the magnetic fields of electrical wires, presenting a novel perspective to address this growing concern. Through a thorough comparative analysis of existing methodologies, we not only highlight the limitations of current approaches but also introduce a more efficient technique. The proposed methodology exhibits promising advantages in terms of energy recovery and device sustainability, paving the way for a more environmentally conscious and resource-efficient IoT ecosystem.

Keywords: Internet of Things · Energy Consumption · Energy Harvesting · Reuse of Energy · Magnetic Field Energy

1 Introduction

The Internet of Things (IoT) represents the Internet's progressive evolution, establishing a network infrastructure that connects numerous devices. This enables them to gather and exchange data, facilitating smart, processed decision-making. It has witnessed an exponential growth in recent years, with billions of devices connected worldwide (see Fig. 1). Our previous research [1] highlighted several key challenges in IoT, such as data management, network connectivity issues, the diversity of IoT standards, and the need for robust device management in distributed and often difficult-to-access environments. In addition, we

S. Zhang and L.-J. Zhang (Eds.): SCF 2024 - ICIOT 2024, LNCS 15427, pp. 66–76, 2025.
https://doi.org/10.1007/978-3-031-77003-6_6

highlighted security and performance issues due to the limited resources of IoT devices. Among these various issues, energy efficiency proved to be a crucial challenge, particularly in terms of managing the power supply to battery-dependent IoT devices. It is on this last point that this paper focuses, proposing an innovative methodology for recharging the batteries of IoT devices using the energy generated by the magnetic fields of electrical wires. According to recent studies [2], the global energy consumption of IoT devices is projected to double within the next decade.

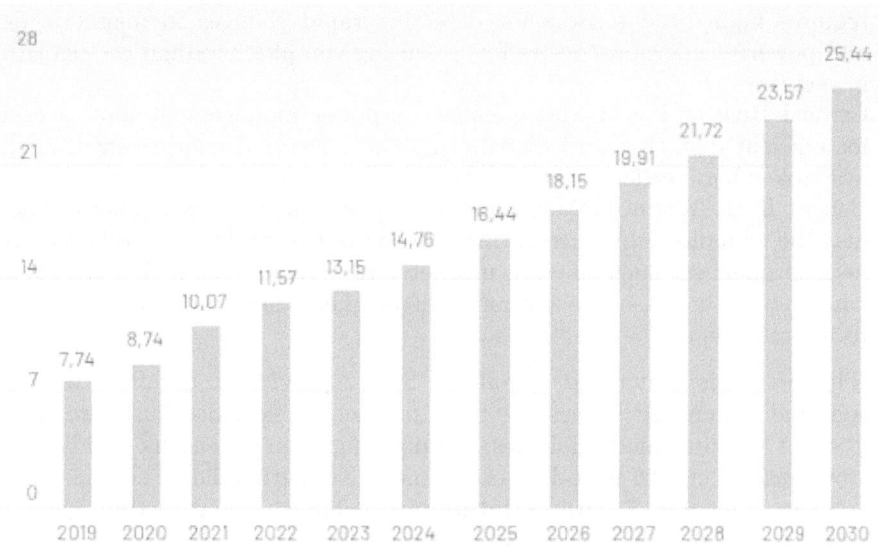

Fig. 1. Growth in the number of IoT devices.

The increasing adoption of IoT devices across industries, ranging from smart homes to industrial automation, underscores the criticality of energy efficiency in sustaining this growth. Furthermore, as these devices become more integrated into our daily lives, the demand for reliable and sustainable power sources becomes even more pronounced.

Addressing the energy consumption of IoT devices is imperative for sustainable technological advancement. By harnessing the energy from magnetic fields, we aim to provide a viable solution to power these devices more efficiently, reducing the strain on existing energy resources.

The proposed methodology not only has the potential to revolutionize the power supply paradigm for IoT devices but also offers wider implications for the broader field of energy harvesting and sustainability. Our main contributions compared to existing methods in IoT area are:

- Higher Efficiency: The proposed methodology can dynamically adapt to changing magnetic fields, which enables it to achieve higher energy extraction efficiency compared to static methods.
- Greater Flexibility: It can be implemented across a variety of form factors and operating environments, making it a more versatile solution for powering IoT devices.
- Improved Reliability: The dynamic nature of the proposed methodology helps mitigate the effects of environmental fluctuations, leading to more reliable and consistent energy harvesting performance.
- Specialized Components: Implementation of the proposed methodology requires high-speed sensors for detecting rapid changes in magnetic fields and powerful microprocessors for executing complex modulation algorithms in real-time.
- Critical Role of Power Management: A power management unit is crucial for efficiently storing and distributing the harvested energy, ensuring it is available when needed.
- Benefit from Advanced Materials: The design of our methodology systems may be enhanced by integrating advanced materials with tailored magnetic properties, such as soft magnetic materials with high permeability, which could increase the efficiency of magnetic field modulation and lead to increased energy extraction.

This article is structured as follows: Sect. 2 provides a detailed theoretical background on energy harvesting from magnetic fields. Section 3 presents an analysis of existing methodologies, highlighting their strengths and areas for improvement. Section 4 introduces our innovative methodology, emphasizing its advantages. The Sect. 5 outlines future implementation and testing while conclusion (Sect. 6) summarizes the key findings.

2   Theoretical Background

The Internet of Things (IoT) is rapidly transforming our world. This section explores its diverse applications, delves into the fundamental three-layer architecture, and briefly explains the function of each layer.

2.1   Internet of Things

The Internet of Things is a concept that refers to the extension of Internet connectivity beyond traditional computing devices such as computers and smartphones to include a variety of everyday objects. These objects, equipped with sensors, software and other technologies, can collect and exchange data with other devices and systems on the Internet. The IoT spans a variety of domains, including home automation, industrial management, healthcare, agriculture and smart cities (Fig. 2. It optimises monitoring, decision-making and operational processes.

Regarding the IoT architecture, many of researches agree on three layers (Fig. 3). They are: Perception layer, Network layer and Application layer.

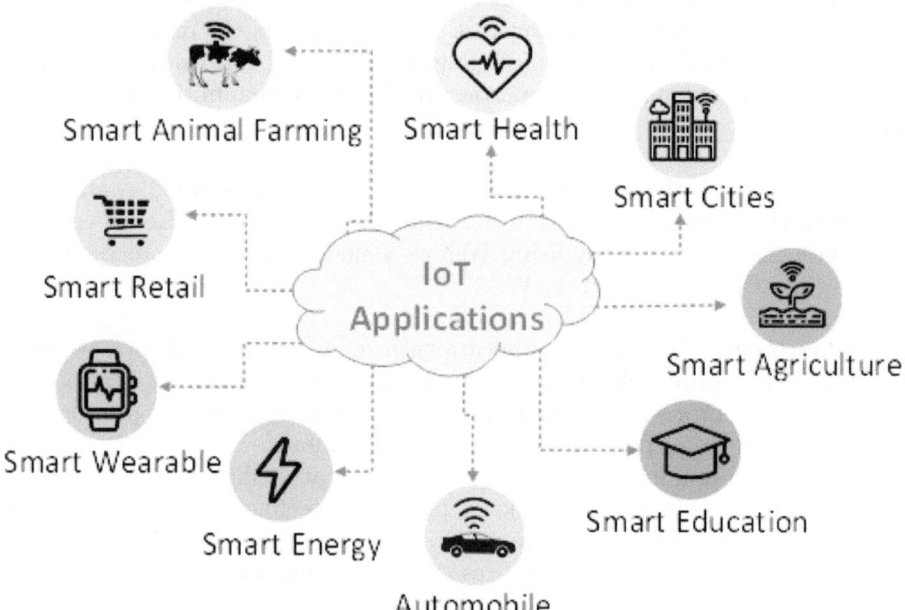

Fig. 2. IoT Application Domains.

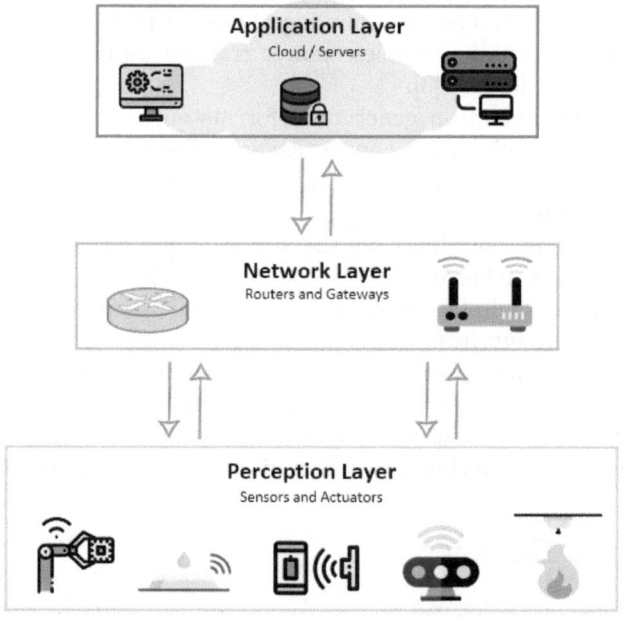

Fig. 3. Three layers of IoT architecture.

Perception Layer: It is first layer in IoT composition. The role of this layer is to collect and send data to the Network layer. It collects the data from sensors which are attached to the various IoT gadgets. There are various types of sensors which sense different physical properties. It also does some initial processing on collected data.

Network Layer: It is the layer placed in between of three tiers in IoT composition. The role of this layer is to route and transmit the data received from Perception layer. Data may be passed by using Web as a media. Various protocols used at this layer are Bluetooth, Zigbee, Wi-fi.

Application Layer: It displays applications to end stakeholders for specialized ambition. For example, Smart Home application, Smart City application. The application layer process the data received from Network layer and produces end result according to purpose of specific IoT application.

The burgeoning number of IoT devices necessitates efficient and sustainable power solutions. This section explores promising technologies and techniques to address this challenge. We examine established methods like electromagnetic induction generators and magnetic resonant coupling, along with the exciting potential of meta-materials for energy harvesting.

2.2   Relevant Technologies and Techniques

Various technologies employ this principle, such as electromagnetic induction generators and magnetic resonant coupling. These technologies find applications in a range of fields including wireless power transfer and energy harvesting for low-power electronic devices [3].

Electromagnetic induction generators, for instance, are widely used in scenarios where a direct electrical connection is unfeasible or impractical. Their versatility in generating power from fluctuating magnetic fields makes them a valuable tool in energy harvesting.

Magnetic resonant coupling, on the other hand, leverages the resonance between two coils to achieve efficient energy transfer [4]. This technique has gained prominence in wireless charging applications, demonstrating the potential for extracting energy from magnetic fields.

Additionally, research has shown promise in utilizing meta-materials to enhance the efficiency of energy harvesting from magnetic fields [5]. These engineered materials exhibit unique electromagnetic properties that can be tailored to specific frequencies, offering new possibilities for energy extraction.

3   Literature Review

This section delves into existing literature on various methods for charging IoT device batteries. We will examine established techniques like electromagnetic induction generators and magnetic resonant coupling, exploring their operating principles, advantages, and limitations (refer to Figures. Following a closer look at each methodology, a comparative analysis will be presented, highlighting the strengths and weaknesses of each approach in the context of IoT device battery charging. This comparative analysis aims to provide insights into the most suitable method based on application-specific requirements.

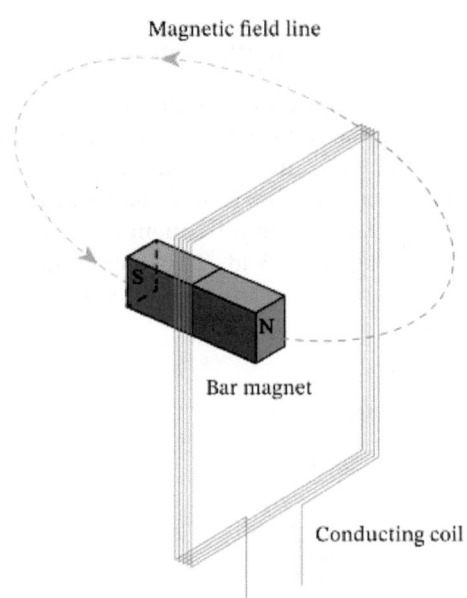

Fig. 4. Illustration of Electromagnetic Induction Generators.

3.1   Method 1: Electromagnetic Induction Generators

Electromagnetic induction generators have been a widely used method for harvesting energy from magnetic fields [6]. These devices consist of coils wound around a magnetic core. When subjected to a changing magnetic field, an EMF is induced, which can then be rectified and stored.

The operational principle of electromagnetic induction generators is rooted in the transformation of magnetic energy into electrical energy (Fig. 4. As the magnetic field surrounding the wire fluctuates, it induces a voltage across the coil. This induced voltage can then be harnessed for various applications, ranging from powering small electronic devices to contributing to larger-scale energy grids.

While this method has demonstrated effectiveness in converting magnetic energy into usable electrical power, it is not without its limitations. Notably, electromagnetic induction generators tend to be less efficient at lower frequencies, necessitating careful consideration of the operating environment and frequency range.

Furthermore, recent advancements have explored the integration of advanced materials, such as superconductors, to enhance the performance of electromagnetic induction generators. These materials exhibit zero electrical resistance, potentially leading to higher efficiency and improved energy conversion.

3.2   Method 2: Magnetic Resonant Coupling

Magnetic resonant coupling is another technique employed for energy harvesting. It involves the use of resonant circuits to maximize energy transfer between coils, enabling efficient power extraction from varying magnetic fields (Fig. 5).

The resonance phenomenon is pivotal in enhancing the efficiency of energy transfer. By carefully tuning the resonant frequency of the coils, maximum power can be extracted from the magnetic field. This technique is particularly advantageous in scenarios where precise control over the energy harvesting process is critical.

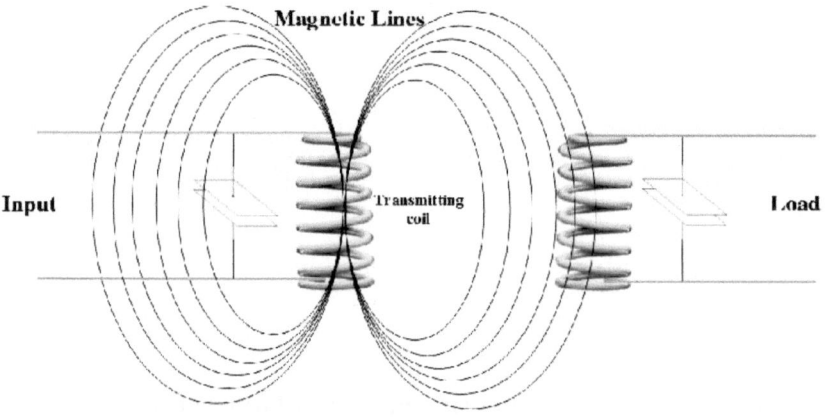

Fig. 5. Illustration of Magnetic Resonant Coupling.

However, it is worth noting that magnetic resonant coupling may require meticulous calibration and maintenance to ensure optimal performance. Deviations from the resonant frequency can lead to decreased efficiency and diminished energy harvesting capabilities.

Recent studies have explored the integration of advanced control algorithms and adaptive tuning techniques to further optimize the performance of magnetic resonant coupling systems. These approaches aim to dynamically adjust the resonance parameters, enabling robust and efficient energy extraction.

3.3   Comparative Analysis

While both methods have proven effective in specific applications, they also exhibit limitations [7]. Electromagnetic induction generators tend to be bulky and less efficient at low frequencies, whereas magnetic resonant coupling requires precise tuning for optimal performance.

When evaluating these existing methodologies, it is crucial to consider the specific requirements and constraints of the intended application. Factors such as frequency range, form factor, and environmental conditions will influence the choice of energy harvesting method.

The selection of an energy harvesting method should be guided by a comprehensive analysis of these factors, as well as a consideration of the long-term sustainability and reliability of the chosen approach.

Table 1. Comparative Analysis of Electromagnetic Induction Generators and Magnetic Resonant Coupling

Comparison Criteria	Electromagnetic Induction Generators	Magnetic Resonant Coupling
Operating Principle	Utilizes coils around a magnetic core to induce voltage	Employs resonant circuits to maximize energy transfer
Efficiency	Effective in converting magnetic energy to electricity, less efficient at lower frequencies	High efficiency in energy transfer through resonance
Applications	Suitable for a wide range of applications from small electronic devices to large-scale energy grids	Advantageous in scenarios requiring precise control of the harvesting process
Limitations	Less efficient at lower frequencies. Requires consideration of the operating environment and frequency range	Requires precise calibration and maintenance for optimal performance
Technological Advancements	Integration of advanced materials like superconductors to enhance performance	Integration of advanced control algorithms and adaptive tuning techniques for optimization
Performance Optimization	Potential for improved efficiency and energy conversion with new materials	Dynamic resonance parameter adjustments enable robust and efficient energy extraction

Table 1 highlights the advantages and areas for improvement of these methods.

4   Proposed Methodology

Our proposed methodology introduces a novel approach, this technique involves dynamically altering the magnetic field's intensity and direction to maximize energy extraction.

The methodology represents a departure from traditional static energy harvesting methods. By actively modulating the magnetic field, we can adapt to changing environmental conditions and optimize energy capture. This dynamic approach holds promise for significantly improving the efficiency of energy harvesting from electrical wires.

4.1   Technical Details and Components

Our methodology utilizes a specialized control circuit to modulate the magnetic field [8]. This circuit interfaces with a sensor array to detect changes in the magnetic field, allowing for real-time adjustments. Additionally, a power management unit ensures efficient energy storage and distribution (Fig. 6).

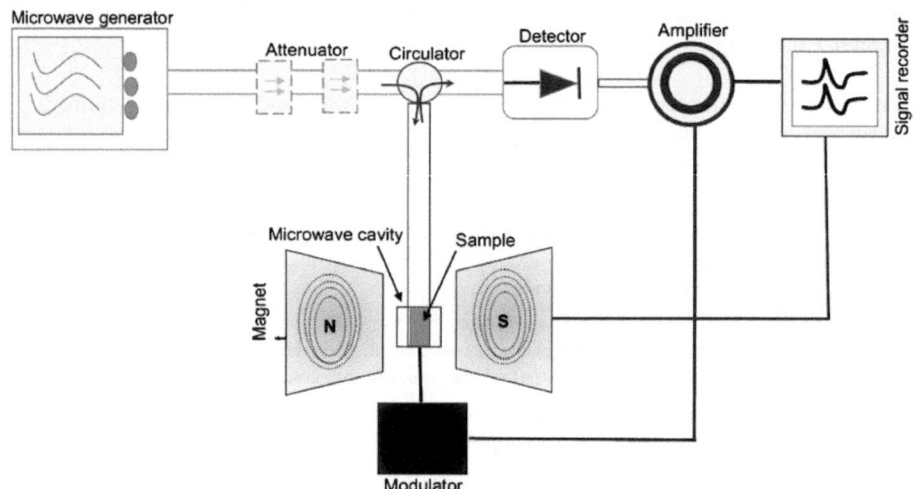

Fig. 6. Illustration of Magnetic Field Modulation.

The control circuit employs advanced algorithms to dynamically adjust the magnetic field modulation parameters. This adaptability enables our methodology to achieve optimal energy extraction across a wide range of operating conditions [9].

To implement the methodology, specialized components are required, including high-speed sensors capable of detecting rapid changes in magnetic fields [10]. Additionally, the control circuit must be equipped with powerful microprocessors capable of executing complex modulation algorithms in real-time [11]. The power management unit plays a critical role in efficiently storing and distributing harvested energy, ensuring it is available when needed.

Furthermore, the design of our systems may benefit from the integration of advanced materials with tailored magnetic properties [12]. For instance, soft magnetic materials with high permeability can enhance the efficiency of magnetic field modulation, leading to increased energy extraction. This integration of materials science into the methodology design represents a promising avenue for further optimization.

4.2   Advantages of the Proposed Methodology

The proposed methodology offers several advantages over existing energy harvesting methods, including:

- Higher efficiency: Our methodology's ability to dynamically adapt to changing magnetic fields enables it to achieve higher energy extraction efficiency than static methods.
- Greater flexibility: The proposed methodology can be implemented in a variety of form factors and operating environments, making it a more versatile solution for powering IoT devices.
- Improved reliability: Our methodology's dynamic approach helps to mitigate the effects of environmental fluctuations, resulting in more reliable and consistent energy harvesting performance.

5   Future Work

The next phase of this research involves the practical implementation of the proposed methodology. A series of experiments will be conducted to evaluate its performance under various conditions, including different wire configurations and magnetic field strengths.

This implementation phase will also include a thorough characterization of our methodology's efficiency and adaptability. Real-world scenarios and environmental factors will be considered to validate its applicability in diverse settings.

Upon obtaining experimental results, a comprehensive analysis will be undertaken to assess the efficiency and reliability of the methodology. Comparisons with existing methodologies will be drawn, providing valuable insights into the practical viability of this innovative approach.

Potential areas for optimization and refinement will be identified, paving the way for further advancements in the field of energy harvesting.

6   Conclusion

This study addresses the escalating energy consumption of IoT devices by leveraging the untapped potential of magnetic fields. We conducted a thorough analysis of existing methodologies, highlighting their strengths and limitations. Our proposed methodology, presents a promising alternative with notable advantages.

The proposed methodology's ability to actively adapt to changing magnetic fields sets it apart from static methods, offering a more efficient and adaptable solution for powering IoT devices. Additionally, our methodology's versatility and reliability make it a well-suited approach for a wide range of applications.

The adoption of our methodology holds significant implications for the IoT industry. It not only promises to enhance the sustainability of IoT devices but also opens up possibilities for new applications in remote or inaccessible environments. By reducing reliance on conventional power sources, our methodology paves the way for a more resilient and eco-friendly IoT ecosystem.

References

1. Guero, A.-M.M., et al.: Challenges and issues for Internet of Things (IoT): recent survey. Math. Model. Comput. **10**(3), 796–806 (2023)
2. Smith, J., et al.: Trends in energy consumption of IoT devices. IEEE Trans. Sustain. Comput. **10**(3), 450–465 (2022)
3. Kim, S., Lee, H.: Wireless power transfer for IoT devices: a comprehensive review. IEEE Internet Things J. **6**(5), 8319–8333 (2019)
4. Lee, W., et al.: Advanced control techniques for optimization of magnetic resonant coupling systems. IEEE Trans. Power Electron. **34**(9), 8981–8991 (2019)
5. Chen, Y., et al.: Magnetic resonant coupling for wireless power transfer: a comprehensive review. IEEE Trans. Industr. Electron. **67**(7), 5612–5626 (2020)
6. Zhang, L., et al.: Superconducting electromagnetic induction generator for enhanced energy harvesting. IEEE Trans. Appl. Supercond. **31**(5), 1–5 (2021)
7. Wang, C., et al.: A comparative study on electromagnetic induction generators and magnetic resonant coupling for energy harvesting. IEEE Trans. Industr. Electron. **67**(11), 9268–9279 (2020)
8. Jin, L., et al.: Tailoring soft magnetic materials for efficient magnetic field modulation in energy harvesting applications. Adv. Mater. **30**(42), 1–9 (2018)
9. Liu, H., et al.: A review of magnetic energy harvesting for wearable electronics. Energy Environ. Sci. **13**(6), 1934–1951 (2020)
10. Wang, Z.L., et al.: Piezoelectric nanogenerators based on Zinc Oxide nanowire arrays. Science **316**(5821), 102–106 (2014)
11. Hu, Y., et al.: Flexible triboelectric nanogenerator. ACS Nano **11**(2), 2563–2570 (2017)
12. Liu, Y., et al.: Emerging energy harvesting technologies for the Internet of Things. Appl. Energy **286**, 116499 (2021)
13. Atzendorf, T.: Recent advances in electromagnetic induction generators for energy harvesting applications. Sensors **16**(11), 1893 (2016)
14. Kurs, A., Karvelas, A., Moffatt, S., Joannopoulos, J.D., Fisher, P.: Magnetic resonant coupling for wireless power transfer: principles and applications. IEEE Trans. Microw. Theory Tech. **55**(4), 1000–1010 (2007)
15. Engheta, N., Medeiros, S.S., Alonso, J.: Energy harvesting from ambient magnetic fields using metamaterials. Phys. Rev. B **87**(14), 144309 (2013)
16. Hannan, M.A., Arebey, M., Zeng, Y., Minarno, A.: A review of battery charging technologies for Internet of Things (IoT) devices. Renew. Sustain. Energy Rev. **81**, 1373–1391 (2018)
17. Pereira, J.M.D., Romero, L., Lorente, S.: Challenges and opportunities for battery charging in the Internet of Things. Electronics **9**(1), 78 (2020)

Optimizing Target Coverage in Wireless Sensor Networks: A Hybrid Differential Evolution and Simulated Annealing-Based Approach

Jonathan Davenport[1]([✉]), Joshua Chikosa[2], and Habib M. Ammari[3,4]

[1] College of Arts and Sciences, Cornell University, 616 Thurston Avenue,
Ithaca, NY 14853, USA
jbdport21@gmail.com
[2] Cockrell School of Engineering, The University of Texas at Austin,
110 Inner Campus Drive, Austin, TX 78712, USA
[3] School of Engineering, Texas A&M International University,
5201 University Boulevard, Laredo, TX 78041, USA
[4] Wireless Sensor and Mobile Autonomous Networks (WiSeMAN) Research Lab,
School of Engineering, College of Arts and Sciences, Texas A&M International
University, Laredo, TX 78041, USA
Habib.Ammari@tamiu.edu

Abstract. In recent years, wireless sensor networks (WSNs) have gained significant attention due to their wide range of applications in monitoring and surveillance. A WSN consists of numerous sensor nodes that can communicate with each other and sense specific targets within their area of deployment. This paper introduces a multi-phase protocol that combines Differential Evolution (DE) and Simulated Annealing (SA) to optimize target coverage in wireless sensor networks (WSNs). The proposed protocol is designed to systematically reduce sensor redundancy while ensuring comprehensive coverage. Through a sequence of well-defined phases, our method achieves significant improvements in coverage efficiency while also activating fewer sensors compared to traditional approaches. Index Terms—Wireless Sensor Networks (WSNs), Target Coverage, Differential Evolution (DE), Simulated Annealing (SA), Optimization, Sensor Deployment, k-Coverage.

1 Introduction

In recent years, research on wireless sensor networks (WSNs) has grown tremendously. A WSN consists of several sensor nodes that can communicate with each other and sense targets within their area. These sensors are characterized by being small in size with limited energy, usually supplied by a battery. These networks are usually used to monitor regions of interest or to detect natural phenomena, threats, etc.

J. Chikosa and H. M. Ammari—Contributed equally to this work.

© The Author(s), under exclusive license to Springer Nature Switzerland AG 2025
S. Zhang and L.-J. Zhang (Eds.): SCF 2024 - ICIOT 2024, LNCS 15427, pp. 77–94, 2025.
https://doi.org/10.1007/978-3-031-77003-6_7

A large issue in WSNs is optimizing sensor node coverage. Coverage optimization aims to improve the percentage of a region of interest that can be covered while minimizing the number of sensors and uncovered regions. Sensor nodes are usually deployed randomly across a given region of interest. This random deployment often results in low overall coverage due to coverage holes. As a result, people have developed methods to efficiently deploy sensors and maximize coverage.

The coverage problem can be divided into two categories: target coverage and area coverage. Target coverage focuses on ensuring that specific points of interest are monitored by at least one sensor. On the other hand, area coverage aims to cover the entire region of interest.

In target coverage, each sensor node is placed to maximize the number of targets it can monitor. Various optimization algorithms, including genetic algorithms, particle swarm optimization, and differential evolution, have been employed to find the most optimal placements for sensor nodes.

Effective target coverage in WSNs can significantly improve the reliability and accuracy of the monitored data. It can lead to better decision-making in critical applications such as disaster management, security surveillance, and precision agriculture.

One specific and increasingly important concept in the realm of WSN coverage is k-coverage. k-coverage refers to a scenario where each target within a WSN must be monitored by at least k sensor nodes. This requirement results in higher reliability and fault tolerance for the network's monitoring capabilities.

It is important to note that deploying/activating N targets across K node positions in a $u \times v$ area is an NP-complete problem. Therefore, the computational complexity of determining the optimal node deployment for a large wireless sensor network (WSN) is exceedingly high when using a brute-force approach. To address this, a metaheuristic method is employed to achieve an approximate solution to the node deployment challenge.

This paper proposes a multiphase method aimed at optimizing sensor deployment in WSNs, where the goals are achieving desired k-coverage and minimizing the number of active sensors. The protocol consists of 2 phases that include sensor deployment and minimum sensor activation. By doing this, the proposed method ensures an efficient WSN deployment.

1.1 Problem Definition

Consider a scenario where N targets are distributed within a $u \times v$ area, monitored by M sensor nodes. The challenge lies in optimally placing and activating these sensors to ensure comprehensive coverage of all targets, while also minimizing the number of active sensors to conserve resources and reduce deployment costs. The problem can be formulated as follows:

- **Objective:** Determine the optimal sensor placements that guarantee each target is covered by at least k sensors (k-coverage), with the fewest sensors activated.

- **Constraints:** Each sensor's range must be maximized to cover as many targets as possible without overlap that would lead to redundancy.
- **Optimization Criteria:** The solution must balance between maximizing coverage and minimizing the number of active sensors, all while following the constraints from sensor ranges and target locations.

1.2   Motivation and Contributions

Wireless sensor networks (WSNs) are increasingly deployed across various fields for monitoring and surveillance, necessitating efficient sensor deployment strategies to ensure robust coverage and connectivity. Traditional methods often face challenges in achieving k-coverage with limited sensors, avoiding redundancy, and minimizing the computational effort required for optimal deployment. This paper introduces a novel approach using a hybrid of Simulated Annealing (SA) and Differential Evolution (DE) algorithms, called DESA, which efficiently addresses these challenges. The main contributions of this research are:

1. **Hybrid Optimization Technique:** By integrating SA and DE, the proposed method leverages the strengths of both to enhance both exploration and exploitation capabilities, leading to more reliable sensor deployments.
2. **k-Coverage with Reduced Redundancy:** The DESA algorithm is effective at activating the minimum number of sensors necessary to achieve desired k-coverage which results in reducing redundancy.

1.3   Paper Organization

The rest of the paper will be organized as follows. In Sect. 2, the related works that were used in the creation of the paper will be discussed. In Sect. 3, an explanation of the network model will be given. In Sect. 4 we describe our proposed method for the problem. In Sect. 5, the results of the proposed algorithm developed will be compared to the effectiveness of other algorithms. The conclusions of this paper will be discussed in Sect. 6.

2   Related Works

Many papers focus on the problem of achieving k-coverage in a WSN using an efficient deployment strategy. None of them use the hybrid algorithm of simulated annealing and differential evolution, however, they can be reviewed to help improve the algorithm proposed in this paper.

Khamlichi et al. [1] use a hybrid algorithm based on the Gradient method and SA, while attempting to use a similar and efficient amount of sensor nodes to ensure k-coverage for targets and m-connectivity for sensors. Yarinezhad et al. [3] and Sixu et al. [9] papers are about solving sensor deployment problems in a wireless sensor network using an improved Particle Swarm Optimization (PSO) algorithm and a cooperative Particle Swarm Optimization algorithm.

Han et al. [4] created a paper that optimizes sensor nodes based on a differential evolution algorithm, in order to maximize coverage area. Rebai et al. [2] propose a genetic algorithm to achieve coverage and connectivity in a WSN. Gupta et al. [5] propose a different genetic algorithm that attempts to minimize the amount of total sensors in addition to attempting to achieve coverage and connectivity. Ju et al. [6] focuses on optimizing the amount of sensors used while ensuring coverage of an area. Bai et al. [7] propose an optimal deployment pattern to achieve both total coverage and 2-connectivity for each value of Rcom/Rcov ratio.

The paper by Potthuri et al. [8] covers a similar topic to the one discussed in this paper. They use a hybrid differential evolution and simulated annealing algorithm, however, they use their algorithm solely in order to improve network lifetime compared to other algorithms. The algorithm they used still has a very similar procedure and can be easily compared to the algorithm discussed in this paper.

3   System Models and Problem Formulation

In this paper, we assume a WSN model in which targets are initially randomly spread throughout a two-dimensional area. Along with this, sensors are static and randomly spread as well. A target can be covered by sensor nodes if it is within the sensing range of the sensor nodes. A sensor node is able to sense more than one target. The data-gathering operations are divided into rounds.

3.1   Assumptions and Definitions

Figure 1 provides a visualization of the sensors used in all of the trials throughout the paper look like. It can be used to help further understand the assumptions used in the paper which are as follows:

- **Homogeneous Sensors:** All sensors are identical in terms of their sensing and communication capabilities.
- **Sensing Range:** The sensing range r_s is the radius of the circular area around each sensor node S within which it can detect targets.
- **Communication Range:** The communication range is assumed to be twice the sensing range, i.e., $2r_s$, forming a disk-shaped area around each sensor node S, and is denoted by r_c.
- **Initial Deployment:** Sensors and targets are randomly deployed in the two-dimensional area.
- **No Obstacles:** There are no obstacles in the deployment area, allowing for unobstructed communication and sensing.
- **Binary Sensing Model:** We use a binary sensing model for the sensors, which is the most simple and ideal sensing model in current WSN coverage models. In binary sensing models if a target is touching a sensor at any point then that target is considered fully covered by that sensor.

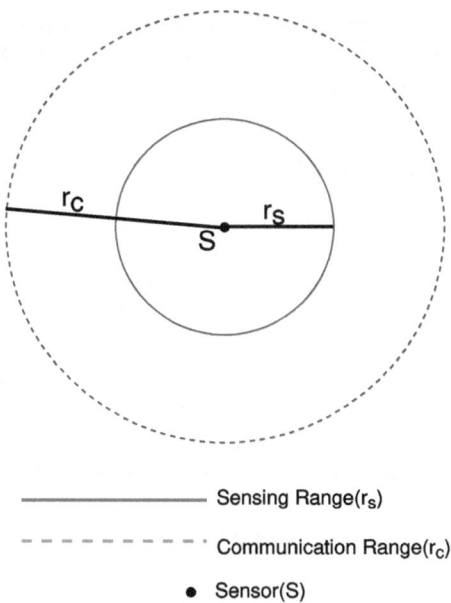

Fig. 1. Example of a sensor

Within a two-dimensional plane, with sensing radius r as the circular radius and sensor node S as the center, for any point $T(x, y)$ of the two-dimensional plane, the mathematical equation of the Binary Sensing Model is as follows:

$$P_{S,T} = \begin{cases} 1 & \text{if } d(S,T) \leq r_s \\ 0 & \text{if } d(S,T) > r_s \end{cases}$$

where $P_{S,T}$ is the probability that sensor node S can detect monitoring point T, r is the sensing radius of sensor node S, and $d(S,T)$ is the Euclidean distance of monitoring point T to sensor node S. The calculation method is as follows:

$$d(S,T) = \sqrt{(S_x - T_x)^2 + (S_y - T_y)^2}$$

where S_x, S_y and T_x, T_y represent the horizontal and vertical coordinates of sensor node S and monitoring point T in the two-dimensional plane respectively. The Binary Sensing Model can simplify the coverage problem and facilitate further research on the problem.

To achieve k-coverage, we must ensure that each monitoring point T is covered by at least k different sensor nodes. Mathematically, for k-coverage at point T, the sum of probabilities of detection by all sensor nodes S_i within range must be at least k:

$$\sum_{i=1}^{M} P_{S_i,T} \geq k$$

where M is the total number of sensor nodes and $P_{S_i, T}$ is the detection probability of sensor node S_i for the monitoring point T. This ensures that the monitoring point T is within the sensing range of at least k sensor nodes.

3.2   Formal Problem Definition

Consider N targets located within a $u \times v$ area that contains M sensor nodes. The objective is to determine the optimal placement and activation of these sensor nodes to ensure that all targets are adequately covered while minimizing redundancy.

Formally, the goals of this paper are:

1. **Reducing Redundancy:** Given the sensing field A of size $u \times v$ and a set of N targets $\{T_1, T_2, \ldots, T_N\}$ located within A, and M sensor nodes $\{S_1, S_2, \ldots, S_M\}$ also deployed in A, the objective is to minimize the number of active sensors while ensuring that each target T_i is covered by exactly k sensors. Mathematically, this can be expressed as:

$$\text{Minimize} \sum_{j=1}^{M} x_j$$

subject to:

$$\sum_{j=1}^{M} P_{S_j, T_i} = k \quad \text{for all } i \in \{1, 2, \ldots, N\}$$

where x_j is a binary variable indicating whether sensor S_j is active ($x_j = 1$) or inactive ($x_j = 0$), and P_{S_j, T_i} is the detection probability of sensor S_j for target T_i defined by the Binary Sensing Model.

2. **Ensuring k-Coverage:** For every target T_i within area A, ensure that it is covered by at least k different sensor nodes. This can be represented by the constraint:

$$\sum_{j=1}^{M} P_{S_j, T_i} \geq k \quad \text{for all } i \in \{1, 2, \ldots, N\}$$

where k is the required coverage level.

4   Proposed Method

This section describes in depth how the simulated annealing and differential evolution algorithms are used in the proposed algorithm.

4.1   Simulated Annealing

Simulated Annealing (SA) is a probabilistic optimization technique inspired by the physical process of annealing in metallurgy, where a material is heated and then slowly cooled to reduce defects and achieve a more stable structure. In optimization, SA uses this concept to escape local optima and explore the solution space more effectively, making it particularly useful for combinatorial problems.

In the context of wireless sensor networks (WSNs), SA is employed to optimize sensor deployment by allowing the algorithm to explore a wide range of configurations initially, before refining the search to focus on more promising regions. This is achieved through the following key components:

4.1.1   Initial Temperature and Cooling Schedule

The algorithm begins with a high initial temperature, set to 100, to facilitate broad exploration of the solution space. As the algorithm progresses, the temperature decreases according to an **exponential decay** cooling schedule:

$$T_{new} = 0.99 \times T_{current}$$

This gradual reduction in temperature decreases the likelihood of accepting worse solutions, allowing the search to focus more on promising areas as the temperature lowers.

4.1.2   Acceptance Probability

Simulated Annealing employs a probabilistic acceptance criterion based on the change in fitness between the current and new solutions, as determined by the Metropolis criterion:

$$P = \exp\left(\frac{\Delta E}{T}\right)$$

where $\Delta E = \text{new\_fitness} - \text{current\_fitness}$, and T is the current temperature. This criterion allows the algorithm to accept worse solutions with a probability that decreases as the temperature decreases, enabling it to escape local optima.

- **Better Solutions:** Always accepted when $\Delta E > 0$.
- **Worse Solutions:** Accepted with a decreasing probability, helping the algorithm explore new regions of the solution space.

Overall, Simulated Annealing provides a balance between exploration and exploitation, enhancing the algorithm's ability to find optimal sensor configurations in WSNs.

4.2 Differential Evolution

Differential Evolution (DE) is a meta-heuristic evolutionary algorithm that excels in achieving global optimization. It is known for its flexibility and simplicity, making it highly adaptable for optimizing sensor deployment in Wireless Sensor Networks (WSNs). DE operates similarly to Genetic Algorithms (GA) as both use evolutionary strategies. However, DE and GA differ in their operation sequences and representations. While GA applies mutation mainly to preserve diversity within the population, DE prioritizes mutation in every generation to enhance offspring quality. The general principle of DE involves three main operations: mutation, crossover, and selection. In the proposed algorithm, evaluation comes after simulated annealing to ensure that the population used will have the highest coverage ratio possible.

4.2.1 Mutation

In DE, mutation involves creating new candidate solutions by adding a weighted difference between two solutions to a third solution. This introduces diversity and explores the search space more effectively. In the context of WSN optimization, the mutation step adjusts the positions of sensors to improve coverage and connectivity.

4.2.2 Crossover

Crossover in DE combines different solutions to generate offspring. This process ensures diversity and helps the algorithm escape local optima by exploring various combinations of sensor positions. The crossover operation is probabilistic, determined by a mutation rate threshold. If the threshold is met, the position is updated; otherwise, it remains unchanged.

4.2.3 Selection

Selection in DE is straightforward. After generating new candidate solutions, the algorithm evaluates their fitness and chooses the best solutions for the next generation. In this algorithm, the acceptance criterion is based on simulated annealing principles, allowing for some exploration of worse solutions with decreasing probability as the temperature decreases.

Tournament Selection
Within the selection process, tournament selection is employed to choose the best and second-best solutions from a subset of the population. By selecting a sample of solutions and evaluating their fitness, the algorithm identifies top-performing individuals who guide the mutation and crossover processes, ensuring that high-quality solutions are favored.

This selection mechanism effectively balances exploration and exploitation by maintaining high-quality genetic material within the population.

4.2.4 Guided Diversification

In addition to standard mutation, guided diversification helps avoid premature convergence by introducing slight random perturbations to the best solutions. This ensures that the algorithm explores new areas in the search space, maintaining diversity and avoiding local optima.

The perturbation rate is set to 0.15, meaning there is a 15% chance of introducing slight modifications to sensor positions.

4.2.5 DE in Algorithm

In this algorithm, Differential Evolution is employed to iteratively refine sensor positions, balancing exploration and exploitation. The adaptive use of mutation, crossover, guided diversification, and tournament selection helps navigate the solution space effectively, enhancing the algorithm's ability to find optimal deployments in complex WSNs.

4.3 Sensor Redundancy Algorithm

In our previous discussions, we outlined the Differential Evolution (DE) algorithm's foundational role in optimizing wireless sensor networks (WSNs). Here, we extend its application to specifically address sensor redundancy, aiming to minimize active sensors while maintaining the required k-coverage.

Algorithm Overview

In this section, we explore the Differential Evolution (DE) algorithm's application to optimizing sensor activation strategies, emphasizing its evolutionary principles. The main objective is to reduce redundancy and ensure efficient energy consumption without compromising network coverage.

4.3.1 Initialization

The first step is the initialization phase. Building on DE's inherent diversity from earlier phases, the initial population includes candidate solutions designed to strike a balance between greedy activation and random deployment. This ensures that the algorithm begins with configurations that are resource-efficient while still capable of achieving comprehensive coverage.

4.3.2 Fitness Evaluation

During the fitness evaluation, the fitness function is enhanced by incorporating a penalty for redundant sensors, thereby prioritizing solutions that achieve k-coverage with the fewest active nodes. This adjustment directs DE's search toward configurations that optimize sensor utilization.

4.3.3 Mutation

The mutation step in this refined DE application focuses on altering sensor activation states to explore configurations with minimal redundancy. By leveraging weighted differences from effective solutions, the algorithm identifies configurations that are less active but still effective.

4.3.4 Crossover

In the crossover step, the algorithm combines high-performing solutions to inherit optimal activation patterns. By focusing on solutions that minimize redundant activations, the crossover operation enhances the quality of offspring solutions in terms of both coverage and efficiency.

4.3.5 Selection

During the selection phase, the algorithm ensures that only solutions with improved sensor activation efficiencies are propagated. By comparing trial vectors to their predecessors, the algorithm continuously narrows down to the most efficient configurations.

4.3.6 Local Search and Repair

A local search and repair mechanism is then employed to further fine-tune solutions, specifically targeting any lingering redundancy. The repair mechanism is adapted to activate the fewest additional sensors necessary to maintain k-coverage, thereby focusing on solutions that require minimal adjustment.

4.3.7 Stagnation and Diversification

Finally, to address potential stagnation and diversification, the algorithm introduces targeted diversification strategies. These strategies allow the algorithm to escape local optima by dynamically adjusting the mutation factor, ensuring continued progress toward optimal sensor deployment configurations.

4.4 Method

The algorithm, depicted in the flowchart shown in Fig. 2, works as follows:

1. **Initialization of Population and Targets:** Targets and Sensor nodes are randomly placed in a $u \times v$ sensing field.
2. **Evaluation of Coverage Ratio:** The coverage ratio is found by dividing the total number of sensors considered fully k-covered by the total number of sensors in the sensing field. For the deployment phase of the algorithm, coverage ratio acts as the fitness function and our goal here is to maximize it.

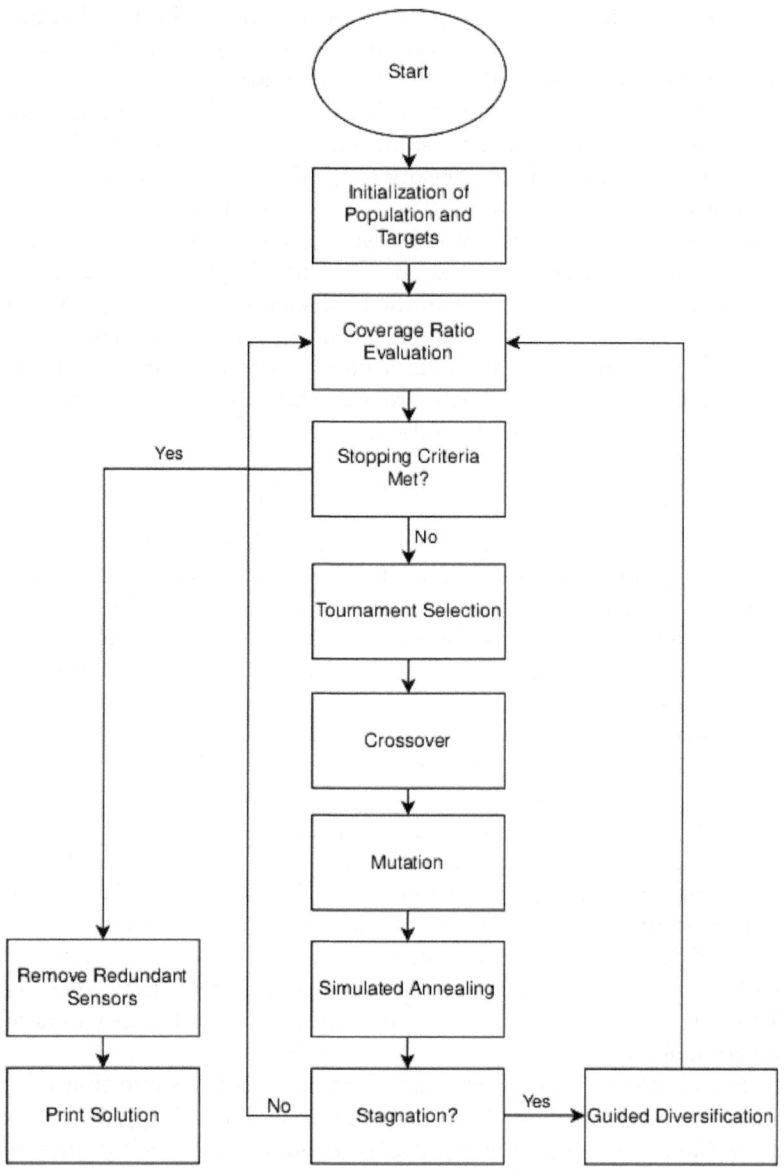

Fig. 2. Proposed Differential Evolution and Simulated Annealing Chart

3. **Checking if Stopping Criteria is Met:** Implemented to ensure the termination of the search process under specific conditions. The search process stops if the maximum number of desired iteration phase been reached, or if the coverage ratio has stagnated for a certain number of iterations.

4. **Tournament Selection:** The process by which the best individuals in a population are selected. In the proposed DE-SA algorithm, it is used to pick the best and second-best individuals in a population.
5. **Crossover:** Involves the combination of genetic information from two or more parent solutions to create a new solution. The formula below demonstrates how the new positions for the sensors are determined. Here, P_{new} is the new position of the sensor, $F1$ and $F2$ are the scaling factors used to determine the influence of the best and second-best sensors over the position of the new sensor. For our algorithm, we use an $F1$ and $F2$ of 1.4 and 2 respectively. P_{best} is the position of the sensor in the best solution, $P_{2nd-best}$ is the position of the sensor in the second-best solution, and P_{cur} is the current position of the sensor. The combined genetic information generates new sensor positions, promoting the exploration of new areas in the solution space and inheriting characteristics from successful solutions.

$$P_{new} = P_{cur} + F1(P_{best} - P_{cur}) + F2(P_{2nd-best} - P_{cur})$$

6. **Mutation:** Introduces random changes to the solution by randomly changing one or more genes to increase diversity. The goal is to explore new areas of the sensing field that may not be reachable by crossover. The mutation rate is set so there is a 10% chance for each sensor's position to undergo mutation after the crossover process, assuming that the sensor is not covering a target. In the proposed algorithm, elitism is used to ensure that the best solutions from the current generation are passed to the next generation. This helps to preserve genetic material and prevents the algorithm from losing the best-found solutions due to crossover and mutation processes.
7. **Simulated Annealing:** Allows the algorithm to accept solutions that are worse than the current solution. This is important for escaping local optima and exploring the sensing field thoroughly. A new solution is generated and if the new solution has a better coverage ratio than the current one, it is accepted. If the new solution is worse, the algorithm calculates an acceptance probability based on the difference in coverage ratio level between the current and new solution and the current temperature. The probability of acceptance is defined as follows: $e^{((P_{new} - P_{cur})/temperature)}$
   where P_{new} is the new position and temperature is the value that determines how likely to algorithm is to accept worse positions. A higher temperature increases the probability of accepting worse solutions, which promotes exploration. As time increases the temperature decreases causing the algorithm to focus more on the best solutions.
8. **Stagnation:** The algorithm checks to see if there has been an improvement in the coverage ratio over a certain amount of iterations. If there hasn't been then the algorithm does guided mutation, and if there is then the coverage ratio is evaluated.
9. **Guided Diversification:** Variation is introduced into the population to allow for more diverse configurations. Overall this helps avoid local optima and increase robustness and adeptness.

10. **Removing Redundant Sensors:** After the optimal solution has been found for all the sensors covering targets, remove the number of sensors that are not needed for the target to achieve k-coverage.

4.5   Time Complexity

The proposed approach involves two main phases: sensor deployment and sensor activation. Each phase has its own time complexity.

4.5.1   Sensor Deployment Phase

This phase optimizes the placement of sensors to ensure adequate coverage and connectivity.

Evaluation: The time complexity for evaluating each sensor configuration is:

$$O(N \times M + M^2)$$

where N is the number of targets and M is the number of sensors.

Main Loop: The overall time complexity for the deployment phase across all iterations is:

$$O(G \times P \times (N \times M + M^2))$$

where G is the number of iterations and P is the population size.

4.5.2   Sensor Activation Phase

After deployment, the activation phase optimizes which sensors to activate for k-coverage.

Table 1. Average Coverage Level for Different Values of k with 25 sensors and 5 targets

	1-coverage	2-coverage	3-coverage	4-coverage	5-coverage
GA	1	1	1	0.904	.872
DE	1	1	1	.996	.956
Proposed DESA	1	1	1	1	1

Table 2. Average Coverage Ratio for Different Values of k with 50 sensors and 10 Targets

	1-coverage	2-coverage	3-coverage	4-coverage	5-coverage
GA	1	1	.98	.936	.868
DE	1	1	1	.996	.916
Proposed DESA	1	1	1	1	1

Evaluation: The time complexity for evaluating each activation configuration is:

$$O(N \times k)$$

Main Loop: The overall time complexity for the activation phase across all generations is:

$$O(G \times P \times (N \times k + M))$$

where G is the number of generations.

4.5.3 Overall Time Complexity

The combined time complexity for both phases is:

$$O(G \times P \times (N \times M + M^2)) + O(G \times P \times (N \times k + M))$$

This reflects the computational effort required for optimizing sensor placement and activation to achieve the desired coverage.

5 Results

In order to see the effectiveness of the algorithm proposed in the paper it was compared to other algorithms designed to achieve target coverage. All of the algorithms tested used the same parameters to ensure proper results.

The tests were run with all of them having the same sensing range, region size, and maximum iterations as shown in Table 1. The only things to change were the amount of sensors, level of coverage, and amount of targets. The results are shown in Figs. 3 and 4 with Tables 1 and 2 showing the specific values that are displayed in the figures. The average coverage ratio value is given for all results to show on average how well an algorithm will do at a certain level of coverage after it has been 25 times.

All of the Algorithms initially started with the targets being in a random location along with all of the sensors or potential sensor positions being randomized. Additionally, they were all run with the same number of iterations. They were run at k-coverage levels, of 1, 2, 3, 4, and 5 and they were run 25 times each to ensure that there were no outlier results. All of the Algorithms were created with the sole purpose of trying to achieve k-coverage. In addition to this, we compared the sensor activation algorithm with another algorithm for the sake of comparison.

Table 3. Test parameters

Region Size	$100\,\text{m} \times 100\,\text{m}$
Sensing Range	$10\,\text{m}$
Maximum Iterations	5000

5.1 Other Algorithms

The other algorithms created were a Genetic Algorithm(GA) and a Differential Evolution algorithm(DE). Both of these algorithms have a different approach to the exploration of a sensing field and Comparing how these algorithms manage in a similar environment can provide insights into which algorithm might perform better under certain conditions in target coverage scenarios, where finding and covering targets is important.

The Genetic Algorithm based on paper [5], simulates evolutionary processes of selection, crossover, and mutation. Each solution undergoes selection, crossover, and mutation to produce new generations. Solutions are selected for reproduction based on their fitness, and exchange portions of their encodings with each other at random points to create offspring, and random changes are introduced to the offspring to maintain genetic diversity within the population. In general, Genetic Algorithms are very useful for finding local optima problems, making them suitable for static target coverage problems.

The Differential Evolution algorithm based on paper [4], starts with a population of candidate solutions. The main operators in DE are also crossover mutation, and selection, however, they differ from a genetic algorithm in how they are operated. In DE, for each member of the population, a mutant solution is generated by adding the weighted difference between two population vectors to a third vector. The mutant vector is mixed with the original vector to create a trial vector, and the trial vector competes with the original vector; if it has a better fitness, it replaces the original vector in the population. DE's straightforward and powerful approach to mutation and crossover makes it highly effective at exploring sensing fields, making it suitable for both static environments (Table 3).

For the sensor activation section of the algorithm, we created a greedy sensor activation algorithm for the sake of comparison. The greedy sensor activation algorithm follows a straightforward heuristic approach, where sensors are sequentially activated based on their individual contribution to coverage until the desired k-coverage is achieved. This method prioritizes activating sensors that cover the most uncovered targets at each step, which can lead to quick coverage with minimal computational overhead. However, it may not always find the most optimal or efficient solution, especially in scenarios with high redundancy or complex target distributions. By comparing this greedy approach with our algorithm, we can better understand the trade-offs between computational simplicity and solution quality, and assess how each method performs under various network conditions and constraints. Additionally, to have a better comparison of the activation abilities of the activation algorithms, the fields in which the sensors are deployed will be densely populated.

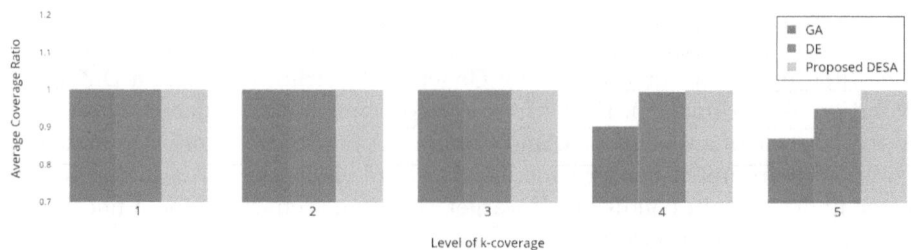

Fig. 3. Average Coverage Ratio measured with 25 Sensors and 5 Targets

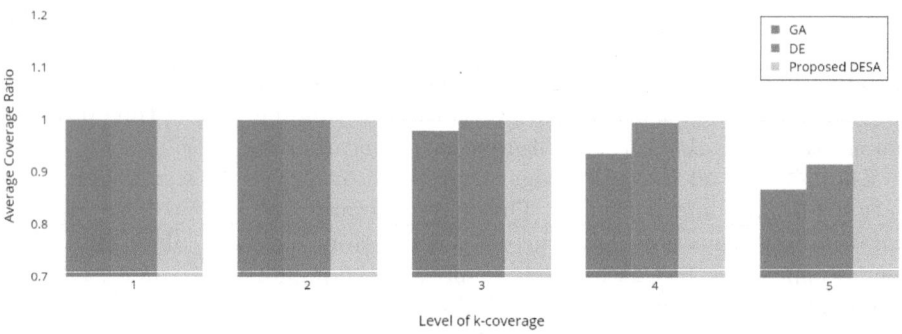

Fig. 4. Average Coverage Ratio measured with 50 Sensors and 10 Targets

5.2   Tests

The first set of tests conducted had the amount of sensors at 25 and the amount of targets at 5. Based on the results the proposed DESA has the best results with it being the only algorithm to achieve full coverage at every single trial attempted with it. The Genetic Algorithm managed to get full coverage when k was equal to 1, 2, and 3, and a coverage ratio around 0.90 and 0.87 when k was equal to 4 and 5 respectively.

The second set of tests had the amount of sensors at 50 and the amount of targets at 10. The proposed DESA managed to get full coverage in all of its trials similar to the first set of tests. The GA Algorithm got full coverage when k equaled 1, 2, and 3, and a coverage ratio around 0.904 and .872 when k was equal to 4 and 5 respectively.

These results show that overall when the amount of sensors and targets increases the coverage ratio increases. This is likely due to there being more overlap in the sensing field with additional targets likely being placed next to each. Moreover, it shows that overall the DE algorithm was more effective than the Ga, and the DESA algorithm was more effective than the GA.

We also evaluated the efficiency of the DESA Algorithm in minimizing sensor activation compared to a Greedy algorithm across different k-coverage levels. The results of the tests can be seen in Fig. 5. The experiments that we conducted

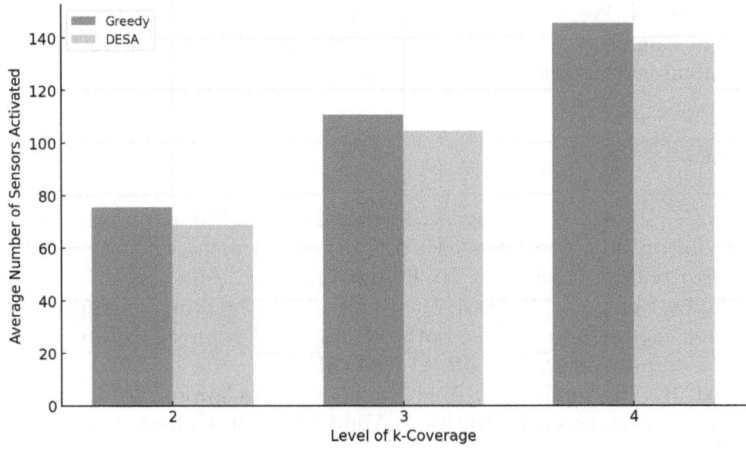

Fig. 5. Average Sensor Activation with 500 Sensors and 125 Targets

were within a field that had 500 sensor nodes and 125 targets. This was done to better show the efficiency of the algorithms due to the high levels of redundancy that happen in densely packed areas. The results show that DESA consistently required fewer sensors activated to achieve the desired k-coverage levels. For 2-coverage, DESA activated 68 sensors on average while the greedy algorithm used 74. For 3-coverage, DESA activated an average of 104 sensors, while the Greedy algorithm activated 110 sensors. For 4-coverage, DESA activated 137 on average while the Greedy algorithm required 147 sensors on average.

These results indicate that DESA is more efficient in minimizing sensor activation while maintaining full coverage, leading to significant energy savings.

6   Conclusions

This study has demonstrated the effectiveness of a hybrid Differential Evolution (DE) and Simulated Annealing (SA) approach in optimizing target coverage in wireless sensor networks (WSNs). By integrating the strengths of both DE and SA, the proposed DESA algorithm has successfully addressed the dual objectives of maximizing coverage while minimizing redundancy and operational costs. The results have highlighted significant improvements in coverage performance compared to traditional methods, with the DESA algorithm achieving full coverage across various levels of required coverage, which is not matched by other tested algorithms. In conclusion, the hybrid approach not only refines the coverage capabilities of WSNs but also contributes to the broader field of network optimization by providing a scalable, efficient solution adaptable to various practical scenarios.

Acknowledgment. We would like to thank the National Science Foundation and the Department of Engineering at Texas A&M University-Kingsville. Both organizations provided invaluable assistance and resources.

References

1. Khamlichi, Y., Tahiri, A., Abtoy, A., Medina-Bulo, I., Palomo-Lozano, F.: A hybrid algorithm for optimal wireless sensor network deployment with the minimum number of sensor nodes. Algorithms **10**, 80 (2017). https://doi.org/10.3390/a10030080
2. Rebai, M., Le Berre, M., Snoussi, H., Hnaien, F., Khoukhi, L.: Sensor deployment optimization methods to achieve both coverage and connectivity in wireless sensor networks. Comput. Oper. Res. **59**, 11–21 (2015)
3. Yarinezhad, R., Hashemi, S.N.: A sensor deployment approach for target coverage problem in wireless sensor networks. J. Ambient Intell. Human. Comput. **14**, 5941–5956 (2023)
4. Han, Y., Byun, H., Yang, B., Kim, J.H., Lee, T.H.: Optimization of sensor nodes deployment based on an improved differential evolution algorithm for coverage area maximization. In: 2019 IEEE 4th Advanced Information Technology, Electronic and Automation Control Conference (IAEAC), Chengdu, China, pp. 250–254 (2019)
5. Gupta, S.K., Kuila, P., Jana, P.K.: Genetic algorithm approach for k-coverage and m-connected node placement in target based wireless sensor networks. Comput. Electr. Eng. **56**, 544–556 (2016). ISSN 0045-7906
6. Yu, J., Wan, S., Cheng, X., Dongxiao, Yu.: Coverage contribution area based k-coverage for wireless sensor networks. IEEE Trans. Veh. Technol. **66**(9), 8510–8523 (2017)
7. Bai, X., Kumar, S., Yun, Z., Xuan, D., Lai, T.H.: Deploying wireless sensors to achieve both coverage and connectivity. In: Proceedings of ACM MobiHoc, Florence, Italy (2006)
8. Potthuri, S., Shankar, T., Rajesh, A.: Lifetime improvement in wireless sensor networks using hybrid Differential Evolution and Simulated Annealing (DESA). Ain Shams Eng. J. **9**(4), 655–663 (2018). ISSN 2090-4479
9. Sixu, L., Muqing, W., Min, Z.: Particle swarm optimization and artificial bee colony algorithm for clustering and mobile based software-defined wireless sensor networks. Wireless Netw. **28**(4), 1671–1688 (2022). https://doi.org/10.1007/s11276-022-02925-x

Research on Automatic Detection and Early Warning of Epilepsy in Electroencephalogram Signals

Shu-xiong Zheng, Si-tong Li, Hui-lin Zhang, and Juan Bao[✉]

School of Public Health, Hubei University of Medicine, Shiyan 442000, China
bao_0203@126.com

Abstract. With the enhancement of computing capabilities at edge computing nodes, edge computing based on cloud computing has seen widespread development and application. In the field of epilepsy prevention and treatment, applications related to edge computing have become very popular. Edge computing is a distributed computing model that places data processing, storage, and application functions at the edge location close to the data source, enabling real-time data processing, reducing data transmission latency, and improving system response speed. The temporal complexity of epilepsy electroencephalogram (EEG) signals has been described and characterized at different time periods. Addressing the multi-channel, high-dimensional, and heterogeneous nature of EEG signals and considering their uncertainty and dynamic characteristics, by analyzing and mining foundational data and combining deep learning theories and methods, epilepsy patients' EEG signals are analyzed and differentiated across multiple time periods, delving into the characteristics of epilepsy EEG signals at different times. In traditional EEG data collection and management systems, cloud storage faces challenges when dealing with large amounts of terminal data, which can reduce real-time data processing performance. To address these issues, this paper proposes an EEG wireless data collection and analysis system based on edge computing. By pushing data processing and storage capabilities to the network edge, data can be processed and analyzed in real-time at the source, thereby reducing data transmission delays and network congestion. Building upon this, the focus is on automatic identification, prediction, and decision-making related to epilepsy, exploring the dynamic patterns of epilepsy automatic identification processes, breaking through traditional epilepsy automatic identification, prediction, and decision-making models, proposing a new method for epilepsy automatic identification, prediction, and decision-making based on "multi-channel fusion - correlation mining - analysis prediction - intelligent decision-making," and transforming the collected information into diagnosis, prediction, and further control of epilepsy seizures. Clarifying the brain mechanisms during epilepsy seizures through EEG signals can provide more references and insights for epilepsy detection research.

Keywords: EEG signal · Automatic detection · Epilepsy prediction · Edge computing

S. Zhang and L.-J. Zhang (Eds.): SCF 2024 - ICIOT 2024, LNCS 15427, pp. 95–107, 2025.
https://doi.org/10.1007/978-3-031-77003-6_8

1 Introduction

Edge computing is a distributed computing paradigm that pushes data processing and storage capabilities from centralized cloud computing data centers to edge devices or edge nodes near the data source. It aims to bring computing resources and data storage closer to the data generation source, the "edge," to more effectively process data and reduce data transmission latency. Edge computing typically involves executing computing tasks on devices, sensors, or local servers near the data source, rather than relying on remote cloud servers.

There is a certain connection and potential application relationship between early detection and recognition of epilepsy and edge computing. Edge computing aims to push data processing and storage capabilities to the network edge, enabling data to be processed and analyzed in real-time at the point of generation, thereby reducing data transmission latency and network congestion. Combining epilepsy signal detection algorithms with edge computing can enhance system real-time performance, security, and efficiency, better meeting clinical needs, and bringing more innovation and possibilities to applications in the medical field.

Epilepsy is a chronic non-communicable disease caused by episodic abnormal highly synchronous electrical activity of brain neurons, and it is one of the most common neurological disorders worldwide. The most common automatic epilepsy detection methods are based on balancing the distribution of sample data during seizure and non-seizure periods for classification and judgment. However, in the actual EEG signals of epilepsy patients, the duration of seizure periods is much shorter than non-seizure periods. Using traditional classifiers to identify epilepsy EEG signals can lead to a bias towards seizure periods in decision boundaries, resulting in increased non-seizure classification space and difficulty in identifying seizure EEG signals. Existing research indicates that the brain patterns of patients change before epileptic seizures. Detecting abnormal changes in neural activity within specific time intervals before seizures can effectively achieve epilepsy warning. Prompt intervention and control by medical personnel upon detecting warning signals, such as medication or electrical stimulation, can reduce the frequency of seizures and improve quality of life, holding significant research significance and clinical value for early intervention and treatment of epilepsy.

Early detection and recognition of epilepsy are of practical significance in delaying epileptic seizures or reducing their harm. Epilepsy detection mainly involves classifying EEG signals during seizure and non-seizure periods to distinguish the different characteristics of epileptic seizure EEG signals from normal EEG signals. This article, combined with the latest research results from domestic and international sources, introduces various epilepsy detection and classification technologies based on EEG. The proposed new methods will provide new perspectives for the detection, classification, and research directions of epileptic seizures.

2   Current Status of Domestic and International Research

Edge computing can play an important role in epilepsy detection. By pushing data processing and analytics functions from centralized cloud computing data centers to edge devices or edge nodes close to the data source, edge computing enables real-time processing and storage of data at the point of generation, thereby reducing data transmission latency. Combining edge computing with EEG data analysis allows for real-time processing of EEG signals near the data source, more effectively handling data and reducing data transmission delays. This helps improve the real-time capability and efficiency of epilepsy detection, bringing more innovation and possibilities to the healthcare field.

EEG records the electrical activity of the brain, which contains potential pathological information and is of great significance for the evaluation and diagnosis, lesion localization, dynamic monitoring, treatment plan, and effect evaluation of epilepsy. Epilepsy detection based on changes in EEG signals is a valuable auxiliary diagnostic and therapeutic means. On the one hand, it can capture subtle changes in brain electrical signals and improve detection efficiency. On the other hand, it can enhance the work efficiency of doctors and provide effective reference diagnoses. This paper introduces EEG-based epilepsy detection techniques and recognition classification techniques from two perspectives.

To date, many traditional and modern methods have been used in the study of epileptic electroencephalogram signals. Epilepsy detection technology based on EEG signal changes contains five stages: acquisition of electroencephalogram data, preprocessing, feature extraction, recognition and classification based on features, and analysis of results. This subsection will introduce the research status at home and abroad based on epilepsy signal detection methods of traditional and modern methods.

2.1   Epilepsy Signal Detection Based on Traditional Methods

In the early 1970s, EEG recordings began to provide support for the diagnosis of epilepsy. Gotman first used half-wave decomposition to process EEG signals, and then extracted three characteristic values of the signal, namely amplitude relative to the background, duration, and coefficient of variation that measures the regularity of duration to detect epilepsy [1]. In the early stage, the detection of epilepsy based on EEG recordings was mainly completed through two techniques: spike detection analysis and seizure analysis.

Linear methods are widely used for epilepsy detection due to their simplicity and adaptability. To detect the preictal state, statistical features such as EEG amplitude and Hjorth parameters are used for seizure detection [2]. Other linear features such as power and signal variance are also used to detect epileptic seizures [3, 4]. In addition, using a linear prediction filter can successfully determine the onset and offset of epileptic seizures [5]. The linear least squares (LS) method is used to preprocess EEG signals to detect epileptic seizures [6]. The interictal peak rate is detected as an indicator of an impending seizure [7].

EEG signals contain low-frequency information for long periods and high-frequency information for short periods. Therefore, time-frequency features are often used for epileptic seizure detection [8, 9]. Wavelet transform (WT) is a technology based on multi-resolution analysis, which is used to capture relevant frequency information at low frequencies and relevant time information at high frequencies. Discrete wavelet transform (DWT) is used to analyze and characterize epileptiform discharges [10]. Power spectral density (PSD) is used as a determination index for dynamic channels of epilepsy detection. To reveal the seizure pattern, researchers have introduced a time-frequency matched filter [11]. Empirical mode decomposition (EMD) and intrinsic mode functions are used to distinguish between interictal and ictal states [12].

2.2 Epilepsy Signal Detection Based on Modern Methods

In recent years, a large number of related studies have proved that the brain is a chaotic dynamical system with complexity and nonlinear characteristics. Based on nonlinear dynamics and chaos theory, nonlinear features such as entropy [13], energy and correlation dimension [14], fractal dimension [15], Lyapunov exponent [16] and higher-order spectra (HOS) [17, 18] are extracted from the detailed and approximate coefficients of wavelet transform to analyze EEG. Using intracranial EEG signals as input, the quantification and evaluation of epilepsy using nonlinear dynamics methods has been verified [19]. The correlation dimension is used to study different neural states of epileptic EEG [20]. Recurrence quantification analysis features have been used for epilepsy detection. Approximate entropy (ApEn) and permutation entropy (PE) [21] are used to distinguish the states of epilepsy.

Epileptic EEG detection algorithms based on traditional feature extraction ignore more hidden feature information inside the brain, thus affecting the accuracy of epilepsy detection. Subsequently, more and more epilepsy detection methods based on machine learning and artificial intelligence have been proposed. At present, methods for detecting epilepsy based on EEG include classification methods such as support vector machine (SVM), naive Bayes, neural network, fuzzy logic system, long short-term memory (LSTM), etc. Agarwal et al. [22] combined CNN with support vector machine (SVM) to propose a CNN-SVM model for epilepsy prediction. The model is deployed in an automatic edge computing service system. The experimental results verify that this is a feasible method for epilepsy seizure prediction.

These methods first extract features from EEG, then use the obtained new features to train the model for classification, and finally use the trained model for detection to realize the function of epilepsy detection. Although many feature extraction and classification methods have been used for epileptic EEG detection, how to extract rich and key features for subsequent effective detection is still an important challenge.

Most of the above epilepsy signal detection methods have the following three problems:

(1) In epilepsy detection research based on EEG signals, features such as the time domain and frequency domain of EEG are usually combined with different algorithms to identify different EEG patterns. Different EEG feature extraction methods and classification methods are time-consuming and labor-intensive and do not meet the real-time requirements in clinical practice.
(2) EEG feature extraction methods are mainly based on single time-frequency analysis, nonlinear dynamics analysis, etc. There are few methods that fuse different types

of features of EEG data for epilepsy signal recognition and classification, and the classification results are not comprehensive.

(3) What classifier should be used to construct a model for the features extracted from the EEG data of epilepsy patients to improve the epilepsy detection level, or how to optimize the performance of the existing classification model to optimize the epilepsy detection results still needs further research.

2.3 Advantages and Applications of Combining Epilepsy Detection with Edge Computing

Combining edge computing technology can provide a more efficient, real-time, and secure solution for the early detection and identification of epilepsy. Combined with the computing power of edge computing, a more intelligent decision-making process can be realized on local edge devices, providing more accurate and timely decision support for medical staff and improving the treatment effect of epilepsy patients.

(1) Real-time performance and low latency: In a clinical setting, real-time performance and low latency are crucial for epilepsy detection. By implementing data processing and analysis on edge devices, real-time monitoring and identification of epileptic seizure signals can be achieved, reducing latency and enabling alarms and interventions to occur more promptly.

(2) Privacy and security: Electroencephalogram (EEG) data of epilepsy patients is sensitive information involving privacy and security issues. By performing data processing and analysis on edge devices, the risk of data during network transmission can be reduced, and data privacy and security can be improved. EEG data of epilepsy patients is privacy-sensitive information that requires high protection. Edge computing can perform data processing on local devices, reducing the risk of data being stolen or tampered with during transmission, thereby enhancing data privacy and security.

(3) Efficient use of resources: By performing partial data processing and analysis on edge devices, dependence on cloud resources can be reduced, network transmission costs can be lowered, and overall system efficiency can be improved.

(4) Intelligent decision-making: Intelligent algorithms deployed on edge devices can make decisions based on real-time data. For example, an alarm can be issued in advance or an intervention measure can be initiated before an epileptic seizure is detected.

(5) Network bandwidth optimization: Edge computing can perform data processing and storage at local endpoints and only transmit necessary summaries or results back to the cloud, thereby reducing the demand for network bandwidth and lowering data transmission costs.

(6) Enabling offline work: Some edge devices may need to work without an internet connection. Deploying epilepsy detection algorithms to edge devices can enable these devices to perform data processing and detection offline, increasing the flexibility of applications. Edge devices usually have a certain ability to work offline and can perform data processing and analysis even in the absence of a network connection. This characteristic enables EEG signal processing and decision-making to still

be performed in some relatively remote medical environments or places with poor network conditions.

Therefore, combining epilepsy signal detection algorithms with edge computing can improve the real-time performance, security and efficiency of the system, better meet clinical needs, and bring more innovation and possibilities to applications in the healthcare field.

3 Research Contents, Research Scheme and Route

3.1 Research Contents

In terms of edge computing, significant portions of the processing of epilepsy EEG signals can be moved to edge devices to reduce data transmission requirements and enhance real-time capabilities. By integrating edge computing, faster decision responses and more effective data processing can be achieved, particularly suited for medical applications that demand high levels of real-time performance. By deploying deep learning models and algorithms on edge devices, real-time analysis and decision-making on epilepsy EEG signals can be carried out locally on the devices. This approach can reduce data transmission latency, lessen reliance on cloud resources, and bolster the system's privacy protection capabilities. Furthermore, combining edge computing can also enhance system reliability and stability. Even in cases of unstable or interrupted network connections, edge devices can maintain the ability to analyze and make decisions on epilepsy EEG signals. Thus, the integration of epilepsy EEG signal processing with edge computing holds the potential to enhance system real-time performance, security, and reliability, offering greater possibilities for epilepsy treatment and management in the medical field.

Centering on the issue of "automatic recognition, analysis prediction and decision-making method research of epileptic electroencephalogram (EEG) signals", from three levels of multi-channel fusion, analysis prediction and intelligent decision-making in big data processing of EEG signals, research on "multi-channel fusion method of epileptic EEG signals based on deep learning", explore new methods of epileptic EEG signal fusion in complex environments, and study "dynamic change rules and analysis prediction methods of epileptic EEG signals based on deep learning", explore new methods of association mining and analysis prediction of epileptic EEG signals, study "epileptic intelligent decision-making method", and explore new decision-making methods for automatic recognition and analysis of epilepsy. The research contents of the thesis are as follows.

(1) Research on multi-channel fusion method of epileptic EEG signals for feature extraction

   Research on methods such as "multi-channel feature extraction" and "multi-channel data perception fusion" to solve the problem of insignificant differences between patients centered on the deep learning model of epileptic EEG signals and difficult classification.

(2) Research on dynamic change rules and analysis prediction methods of epileptic EEG signals by deep learning

Thoroughly analyze the structural characteristics of deep learning network models and expand them to epileptic EEG signal modeling. Research and design deep neural network structures with autonomous learning characteristics and optimization methods for generating related parameters and weights, and research on improved methods for bioinformation analysis and prediction.

(3) Research on intelligent decision-making methods

Study the design pattern of "analysis prediction + intelligent decision-making" to optimize the performance of the epileptic EEG signal system. The intelligent decision-making system includes functions such as data processing, acquisition of classification rules, model evaluation, and disease prediction.

3.2 Research Scheme

In the field of edge computing, a transformative paradigm is emerging, namely the relocation of the processing of multi-channel EEG signals from epileptic patients to edge devices. This migration not only helps reduce data transmission requirements but also enhances the immediacy of signal analysis. By leveraging the capabilities of edge computing, the fundamental principles of feature extraction for multi-channel EEG signals are directly applied to edge devices, facilitating the seamless integration of various data streams. Research endeavors cleverly employ methods such as "multi-channel feature extraction" and "multi-channel data perception fusion" to optimize the processing of multi-channel epileptic EEG signals in a dynamic edge computing environment.

(1) In the realm of edge computing, a pivotal shift can occur by relocating the processing of multi-channel EEG signals from epileptic patients to edge devices. This transition not only reduces data transmission requirements but also amplifies real-time capabilities. Harnessing the potential of edge computing empowers the application of feature extraction principles to multi-channel EEG signals directly at the edge devices, facilitating the amalgamation of data streams. Research endeavors delve into methodologies like "multi-channel feature extraction" and "multi-channel data perception fusion," aimed at refining the processing of multi-channel epileptic EEG signals within the edge computing environment.

(2) The deployment of dynamic deep learning methodologies on edge devices presents a promising avenue for real-time analysis and predictive insights into epileptic EEG signals. By embedding deep learning models onto edge devices, the computational prowess of edge computing can be harnessed to address the dynamic nature of epileptic EEG signal patterns and their predictive analytics needs. Crafting deep neural network architectures with autonomous learning capabilities and optimization techniques becomes paramount in the pursuit of multi-channel EEG signal analysis and prediction within edge environments.

(3) The integration of an intelligent decision-making system with edge computing infrastructure opens up avenues for real-time analysis and decision-making concerning epileptic EEG signals on edge devices. The harmonization of predictive analytics with intelligent decision-making serves to enhance the processing capabilities of epileptic EEG signals on edge devices. The culmination of this integration manifests in the establishment of an epileptic EEG signal early warning system operational on

edge devices. This comprehensive system encompasses stages such as data processing, rule acquisition, model evaluation, and seizure prediction, effectively addressing the variability and intricacy inherent in EEG signals. Leveraging datasets from the University of Bonn in Germany and the Boston Children's Hospital in the United States for multi-classification detection research further substantiates the efficacy and feasibility of the system within the edge computing environment.

3.3   Overall Research Route

First of all, there is a certain connection and potential application relationship between the early detection and identification of epilepsy and edge computing. Edge computing is a distributed computing paradigm that aims to push data processing and storage capabilities to the edge of the network, enabling data to be processed and analyzed in real time at the place where it is generated, thereby reducing data transmission latency and network congestion.

In the traditional EEG data acquisition and management system, when the amount of data at the terminal is large, cloud storage will face challenges and reduce the real-time performance of data processing. In addition, centralized transmission of data also has higher requirements for the bandwidth of the transmission network and will consume huge bandwidth and computing resources. Frequent access by users to the cloud will increase network traffic and cause service interruptions.

To solve the related problems under the traditional cloud computing model, this paper proposes the EEG wireless data acquisition and analysis model based on edge computing as shown in Fig. 1. In this mode, edge nodes are set up in the acquisition area, and edge-end devices use their certain computing resources to migrate some tasks from the cloud center to the edge end for execution. Therefore, the introduction of edge nodes can effectively reduce the dependence on the computing center.

On the one hand, the electroencephalogram (EEG) data of epilepsy patients is sensitive information, involving privacy and security issues. By performing data processing and analysis on edge devices, the risk of data during network transmission can be reduced, and data privacy and security can be improved. Edge computing can process data on local devices, reducing the risk of data being stolen or tampered with during transmission, thereby enhancing data privacy and security.

On the other hand, some edge devices may need to work without an internet connection. Deploying epilepsy detection algorithms to edge devices enables these devices to perform data processing and detection in an offline state, increasing the flexibility of applications. Edge devices usually have a certain offline working ability and can perform data processing and analysis even in the absence of network connections. This characteristic enables EEG signal processing and decision-making to still be carried out in some medical environments that are relatively remote or have poor network conditions.

Next, it is necessary to address the processing and analysis methods of epileptic electroencephalogram (EEG) signals for early warning tasks. Artificial intelligence and machine learning have gradually formed a complete theoretical system and methods, and relevant theoretical and applied achievements can be used as references for this paper's research. The technical route of this paper is as follows: adopting comprehensive planning and implementing it step by step, with applied basic research as the research

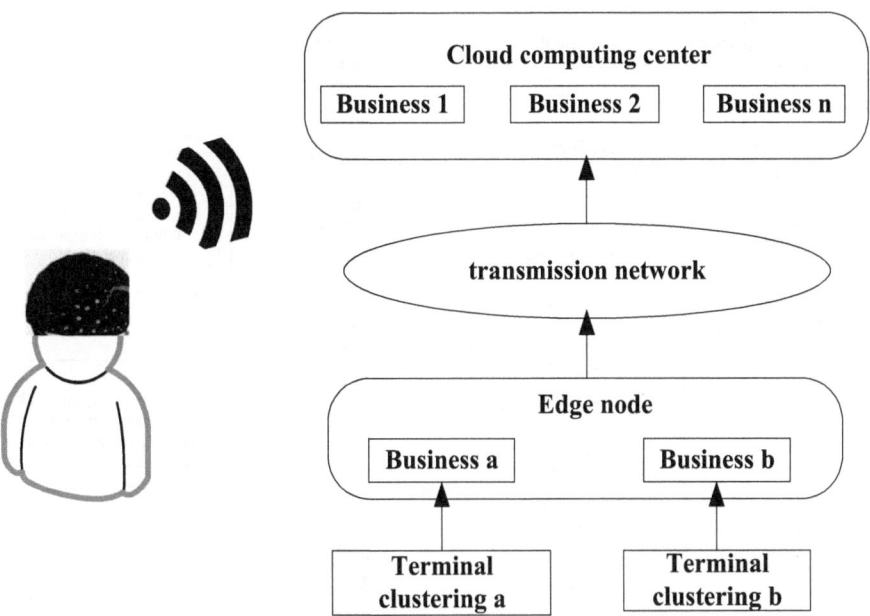

Fig. 1. Cloud computing and edge computing model

objective, focusing mainly on innovation, supplemented by tracking research methods, and studying the automatic identification, early warning, and decision-making methods of epileptic EEG signals based on deep learning. The technology route is shown in Fig. 2.

The complexity of the time series of epileptic electroencephalogram (EEG) signals is characterized and described in different periods. For multi-channel, high-dimensional, and heterogeneous EEG signals, considering their uncertain and dynamic characteristics, analyzing and mining basic data, and utilizing deep learning theories and methods, analyzing and distinguishing the EEG signals of epileptic patients in multiple periods, and deeply mining the characteristics of epileptic EEG signals in multiple different periods. Based on this, focusing on the issues of automatic recognition, prediction, and decision-making of epilepsy, mining the dynamic change rules of the automatic recognition process of epilepsy, breaking through the traditional automatic recognition, prediction, and decision-making mode of epilepsy, proposing a new method of automatic recognition, prediction, and decision-making of epilepsy based on the "multi-channel fusion - association mining - analysis prediction - intelligent decision-making" mode, and transforming the collected information into diagnosis, prediction, and further control of epileptic seizures.

The introduction of edge computing can optimize the process of epilepsy detection and treatment. By implementing partial data processing and analysis on edge devices, dependence on the cloud center can be reduced, data processing time can be shortened, and network transmission delays can be reduced. This architecture also helps enhance the security and privacy of data, as sensitive information can be processed on local devices

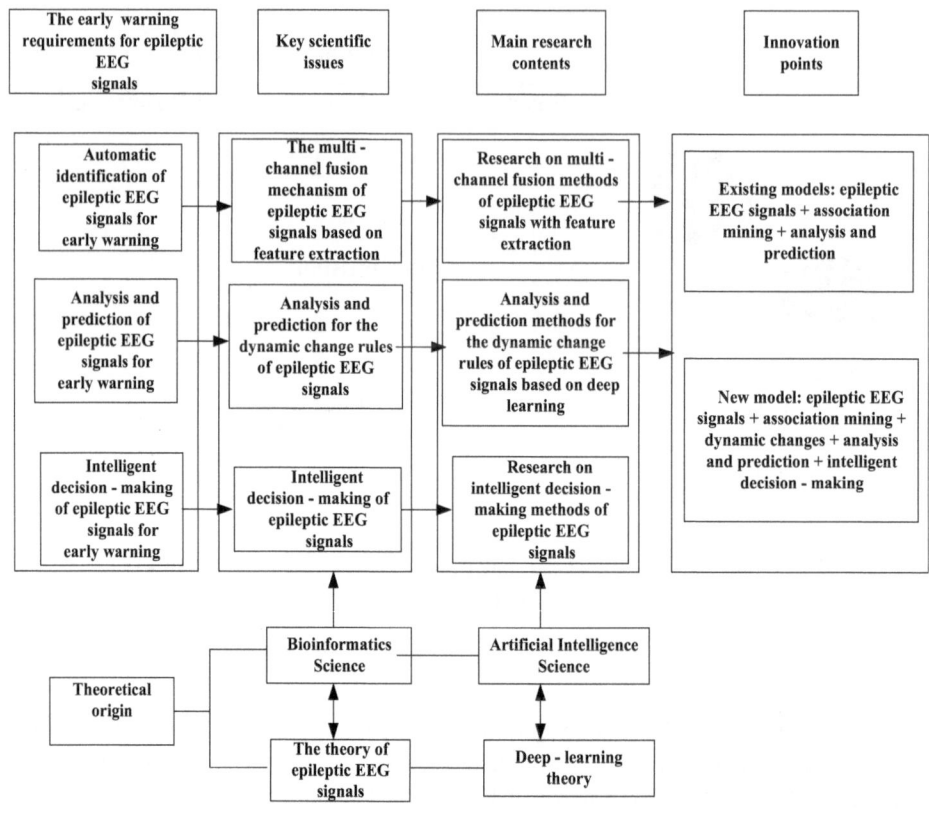

Fig. 2. Technology route

without the need for network transmission. Therefore, combining edge computing technology can more efficiently achieve automatic identification and decision-making of epileptic EEG signals.

4   Conclusion

The epilepsy warning task based on EEG signal analysis algorithms combined with edge computing technology aims to address the challenges of deep learning algorithms in clinical applications. By studying the stability and complexity classification of epilepsy EEG signals, the goal is to provide a faster and more accurate warning system to reduce the impact of epilepsy seizures on patients. By exploring the characteristics of pre-seizure signals in epilepsy episodes, coupled with the real-time and low-latency properties of edge computing, real-time monitoring and analysis of signal dynamics can be achieved. This research introduces innovative aspects such as multi-channel data fusion mechanisms, analysis of dynamic change patterns, optimization of intelligent decision-making methods, and an epilepsy detection model under edge computing, offering new perspectives and methodologies to enhance the efficiency and accuracy of epilepsy warning systems.

(1) Multi-channel data fusion mechanism of epileptic electroencephalogram signals based on feature extraction

As the complexity of epileptic electroencephalogram signals increases, existing analysis methods are difficult to accurately identify and give warnings. This thesis starts with the data generated in the process of automatic epilepsy recognition and analysis, and studies the fusion method between multi-channel data of epileptic electroencephalogram signals, providing a basic theoretical basis for subsequent automatic epilepsy recognition analysis and prediction.

(2) Dynamic change rules and analysis and prediction methods of epileptic electroencephalogram signals

The "multi-channel fusion-association mining-analysis prediction-intelligent decision-making" mode proposed in this thesis is to improve the automatic epilepsy recognition analysis and accurate prediction, and compare it with the decision-making goal to continuously optimize the automatic epilepsy recognition process. However, accurate analysis and prediction depend on the dynamic change rules of epileptic electroencephalogram signals. Therefore, mining the dynamic change rules and prediction of the automatic epilepsy recognition analysis process is another key issue that needs to be broken through in clinical practice.

(3) Intelligent decision-making method

Automatic epilepsy recognition and decision-making are mainly to achieve optimized processing and analysis of epileptic electroencephalogram signals. The intelligent decision-making system includes data processing, classification acquisition, model evaluation, disease prediction, etc., which can overcome the variability and high complexity of signals from different channels, and also retain subtle differences, and finally achieve accurate diagnosis of epileptic electroencephalogram signals.

Application of warning methods in clinical practice, research on the analysis and detection of epileptic electroencephalogram signals in different periods is carried out, and finally the warning task of epileptic electroencephalogram signals is completed.

(4) Epilepsy detection combined with edge computing

In the traditional EEG data acquisition and management system, when the amount of data at the terminal is large, cloud storage will face challenges and reduce the real-time performance of data processing. To solve the related problems, this paper proposes the EEG wireless data acquisition and analysis model based on edge computing. Push data processing and storage capabilities to the edge of the network, so that data can be processed and analyzed in real time at the place where it is generated, thereby reducing data transmission latency and network congestion.

Based on the electroencephalogram (EEG) signals of epilepsy, this paper conducts research on the clinical early warning task of epilepsy. Aiming at the problems of large differences in the recognition results of analysis algorithms for multiple classification tasks due to insufficient characterization ability of epilepsy signals, high complexity of detection models and the need for manual experience to select features, and low universality of algorithms leading to difficulties in the application of early warning methods in clinical practice, research on the analysis and detection of epileptic EEG signals in different periods is carried out, and finally the early warning task of epileptic EEG signals is completed. Taking the actual clinical needs as the core idea and centering on the main problems existing in the clinical application of current epileptic EEG detection algorithms, explore stable, efficient and EEG signal analysis and detection algorithms that conform to the concept of clinical application.

Acknowledgements. This work was supported by the Start-up Foundation of Hubei University of Medicine [No. 2019QDJRW02]; Cooperative Education Program of the Ministry of Education [No. 202101142004]; Innovation and Entrepreneurship training program for students of Hubei University of Medicine [No. S202210929037]. Innovation and Entrepreneurship training program for students of Hubei University of Medicine [No. S202410929019]. Many thanks also to corresponding author Bao Juan for her support of this paper.

References

1. Gotman, J.: Automatic recognition of epileptic seizures in the EEG. Electroencephalogr. Clin. Neurophysiol. **54**(5), 530–540 (1982)
2. Niknazar, H., Mousavi, S.R., Niknazar, M., et al.: Performance analysis of EEG seizure detection features. Epilepsy Res. **167**, 106483 (2020)
3. Van Drongelen, W., Nayak, S., Frim, D.M., et al.: Seizure anticipation in pediatric epilepsy: use of Kolmogorov entropy. Pediatr. Neurol. **29**(3), 207–213 (2003)
4. Mcsharry, P.E., Smith, L.A., Tarassenko, L.: Comparison of predictability of epileptic seizures by a linear and a nonlinear method. IEEE Trans. Biomed. Eng. **50**(5), 628–633 (2003)
5. Altunay, S., Telatar, Z., Erogul, O.: Epileptic EEG detection using the linear prediction error energy. Expert Syst. Appl. **37**(8), 5661–5665 (2010)
6. Roshan, Z.Z.: Detection of epileptic seizure in EEG signals using linear least squares preprocessing. Comput. Methods Programs Biomed. **133**, 95–109 (2016)
7. Gotman, J.: Noninvasive methods for evaluating the localization and propagation of epileptic activity. Epilepsia **44**, 21–29 (2003)
8. Musselman, M., Djurdjanovic, D.: Time–frequency distributions in the classification of epilepsy from EEG signals. Expert Syst. Appl. **39**(13), 11413–11422 (2012)
9. Zhou, M.: Research on the Application of Complexity and Time-Frequency Analysis in the Diagnosis and Seizure Prediction of Epileptic EEG Signals. Taiyuan University of Technology (2019)
10. Adeli, H., Zhou, Z., Dadmehr, N.: Analysis of EEG records in an epileptic patient using wavelet transform. J. Neurosci. Methods **123**(1), 69–87 (2003)
11. Khlif, M.S., Mesbah, M., Boashash, B., et al.: Multichannel-based newborn EEG seizure detection using time-frequency matched filter. Annu. Int. Conf. IEEE Eng. Med. Biol. Soc. **2007**, 1265–1268 (2007)
12. Lopes, M.A., Zhang, J., Krzemiński, D., et al.: Recurrence quantification analysis of dynamic brain networks. Eur. J. Neurosci. **53**(4), 1040–1059 (2021)
13. Zarei, A., Asl, B.M.: Automatic seizure detection using orthogonal matching pursuit, discrete wavelet transform, and entropy based features of EEG signals. Comput. Biol. Med. **131**, 104250 (2021)
14. Fraser, B.A., Wachowiak, M.P., Wachowiak-Smolikova, R.: Time-delay lifts for physiological signal exploration: an application to ECG analysis. In: Electrical & Computer Engineering (2017)
15. Acharya, U.R., Sree, S.V., Suri, J.S.: Automatic detection of epileptic EEG signals using higher order cumulant features. Int. J. Neural Syst. **21**(5), 403–414 (2011)

16. Yakovleva, T.V., Kutepov, I.E., Karas, A.Y., et al.: EEG analysis in structural focal epilepsy using the methods of nonlinear dynamics (lyapunov exponents, lempel-ziv complexity, and multiscale entropy). ScientificWorldJournal **2020**, 8407872 (2020)
17. Khoshnevis, S.A., Sankar, R.: Applications of higher order statistics in electroencephalography signal processing: a comprehensive survey. IEEE Rev. Biomed. Eng. **13**, 169–183 (2020)
18. Feng, Z., He, Q., Wu, B., et al.: Application of biomedical signal processing based on high-order statistics analysis. Chin. J. Med. Phys. **28**(05), 2899–2903 (2011)
19. Pijn, J.P., Velis, D.N., van der Heyden, M.J., et al.: Nonlinear dynamics of epileptic seizures on basis of intracranial EEG recordings. Brain Topogr. **9**(4), 249–270 (1997)
20. Jing, H., Takigawa, M.: Topographic analysis of dimension estimates of EEG and filtered rhythms in epileptic patients with complex partial seizures. Biol. Cybern. **83**(5), 391–397 (2000)
21. Nicolaou, N., Georgiou, J.: Detection of epileptic electroencephalogram based on permutation entropy and support vector machines. Expert Syst. Appl. **39**(1), 202–209 (2012)
22. Agarwal, P., Wang, H.C., Srinivasan, K., et al.: Epileptic seizure prediction over EEG data using hybrid CNN-SVM model with edge computing services. In: Proceedings of the 22nd International Conference on Circuits, Systems, Communications and Computers, Ajorca, 14–17 July 2018, p. 03016. Paris: EDP Sciences (2018)

Cross-Scale Bilevel Aggregation for Multi-exposure Fusion via Conditional Generative Adversarial Network

Longchun Wang[1,2], Mali Yu[1,2,3(✉)], Hai Zhang[1], Taojun Yang[1],
Qingming Leng[4], Xiwei Dong[1,3], Jingjuan Guo[1,3], and Guangxing Wang[1,3]

[1] School of Computer and Big Data Science, Jiujiang University, Jiujiang 332005,
People's Republic of China
maliyu@jju.edu.cn
[2] School of Information Management, Jiangxi University of Finance and Economics,
Nanchang 330013, People's Republic of China
[3] Jiujiang Engineering Research Center for Collaborative Cyber Security Protection,
Jiujiang 332005, People's Republic of China
[4] School of Electronic and Information Engineering, Jiujiang University, Jiujiang
332005, People's Republic of China

Abstract. The aim of multi-exposure fusion (MEF) is to generate a
high-dynamic-range-like image from images captured by common cameras under different exposure settings. The existing generative adversarial network (GAN)-based MEF methods have achieved fair performance. However, when addressing extremely exposed images, these existing GAN-based MEF methods still face numerous limitations, such as
detail loss and unnatural visual effects, partly due to their inability to
sufficiently aggregate multiscale context information. To address these
limitations, we propose a cross-scale bilevel aggregation-based conditional generative adversarial network (CBA-cGAN). The generator contains two subnetworks: a cross-scale aggregation GhostNetV2 (CSA-
GhostNetV2) for capturing and integrating multiscale context information with long-range dependencies and a U-shaped local network (ULN)
for extracting local features. To fully aggregate short-range and multiscale long- range dependencies, we propose the use of bilevel aggregation in CSA-GhostNetV2: intrablock and interblock aggregation. The
intrablock aggregation scheme based on dilated convolution and Ghost-
BlockV2 is designed to aggregate multiscale context information and
long-range relationships. The interblock aggregation scheme is designed
to balance local and global contextual information during the fusion
process by combining features acquired from CSA-GhostNetV2 and the
ULN. Additionally, to better align the visual effect with human perception, we take the average of the input images for the discriminator.
We compare the performance of the proposed method with that of traditional and deep learning methods on two publicly available datasets
in terms of six objective metrics. Extensive experiments are conducted
to demonstrate that the proposed CBA-cGAN outperforms the existing state-of-the-art methods in retaining local details while preserving
overall visual effects.

S. Zhang and L.-J. Zhang (Eds.): SCF 2024 - ICIOT 2024, LNCS 15427, pp. 108–131, 2025.
https://doi.org/10.1007/978-3-031-77003-6_9

Keywords: Multi-exposure fusion · Conditional generative adversarial network · Cross-scale aggregation · Long-range dependency · Interblock aggregation

1   Introduction

Luminance levels differ greatly in the natural world. For example, the illumination in a sunlit environment is several orders of magnitude greater than that in a starlit environment. A common camera cannot capture scenes with very wide dynamic ranges. Therefore, images captured with a single shot always have overexposed or underexposed regions. High-dynamic-range (HDR) imaging is a technique that renders richer brightness and color detail by extending the dynamic range of an image [54]. Aggarwal et al. [1] and Tumblin et al. [49] proposed HDR cameras, which are difficult to use widely because of their high costs. Therefore, researchers prefer software techniques. Although an HDR image can be reconstructed from a single image via enhancement [22,56] or inverse tone mapping [6,8], the limited image information acquired from a single image makes it challenging to recover large saturated regions. A sequence of images with different exposure levels can provide rich information, and multi-image-based methods, known as multi-exposure fusion (MEF) approaches, are dominant. Traditional

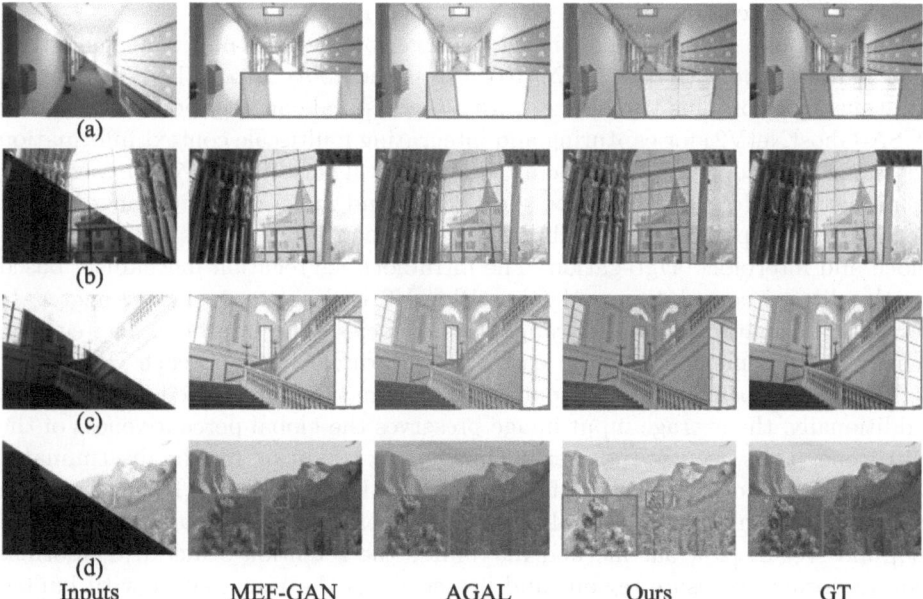

Inputs   MEF-GAN   AGAL   Ours   GT

Fig. 1. Comparative visualization of the multi-exposure image fusion results obtained by different methods on the SICE dataset [4]. Our method maximizes the retention of detailed information in normal exposure regions, and the visual effect aligns more with human perception.

MEF methods typically use handcrafted features, such as pixel features [51,61] and patch features [33,67], to define weight maps or handcrafted fusion rules, such as multiscale transforms [26,63]. Thus, these methods are time-consuming and unsuitable for diverse and complex scenes.

With the wide application of deep learning (DL), various promising networks, such as convolutional neural networks (CNNs) [14,32,52], and generative adversarial networks (GANs) [60,65], have been integrated into MEF and achieved fair performance. However, color distortions and detail losses remain when conducting fusion in cases with extreme exposure, mainly because the convolution operations for extracting features ignore long- range dependencies [10,52]. Some recent studies [18,20,28] have attempted to utilize attention mechanisms to capture global features and combine them with local features to provide improved quality. However, these methods work at a single scale and lack sufficient understanding of the underlying context. Thus, external postprocessing is required to correct global color and local details. Xu et al. [60] and Yang et al. [64] proposed GAN- based MEF networks, which preserve clear details and rich colors via the game played between the generator and discriminator. To enhance textures, Liu et al. [28] extracted edges, merged them with image features in a generator, and added local patch information in a discriminator. Nonetheless, GANs often suffer from pattern collapse, leading to detail losses and unsatisfactory visual effects in the fused results [3]. Thus, these methods still have difficulties in addressing extremely exposed images, due to their inability to sufficiently aggregate multiscale context information.

We propose a cross-scale bilevel aggregation-based conditional generative adversarial network (CBA-cGAN) to address the above issues. The core part of the generator contains two subnetworks: a cross-scale aggregation GhostNetV2 (CSA-GhostNetV2) for capturing and integrating multiscale context information with long-range dependencies and a U-shaped local network (ULN) for extracting local features. To fully aggregate short-range and multiscale long-range dependencies, we propose the use of bilevel aggregation in CSA-GhostNetV2: intrablock and interblock aggregation. The intrablock aggregation mechanism based on the dilated convolution and GhostBlockV2 is designed to better aggregate context information with long-range dependencies. The interblock aggregation scheme is implemented between each CSA-GhostBlockV2 and each ULN block to balance the local and global contextual information during the fusion process. Additionally, the average input image preserves the global perceptiveness of the real scene. Thus, we use the average image as a condition for the discriminator to improve the overall visual effect of the fused image. Figure 1 shows that in comparison with those produced by two GAN-based MEF methods MEF-GAN [60] and AGAL [28], our method maximizes the retention of detailed information in normal exposure regions and better aligns the visual effect with human perception. The following lists the efforts made by our work.

1) We propose a cross-scale bilevel aggregation-based conditional generative adversarial network to effectively aggregate short- and long-range dependencies. The average input image effectively enhances the global visual effect of the fused image.
2) We propose combining dilated convolutions with possessing multiple dilation rates with GhostNetV2 to aggregate multiscale context information and long-range relation- ships.
3) We propose an interblock aggregation scheme to balance local and global contextual information during the fusion process by combining features acquired from CSA- GhostNetV2 and the ULN.
4) Extensive experiments are conducted on two public datasets, showing that the pro- posed model outperforms the existing state-of-the-art methods in terms of retaining local details while preserving overall visual effects.

The remainder of this work is organized as follows. In Sect. 2, we discuss the development of traditional and DL-based MEF methods and networks related to our methods. In Sect. 3, we describe the working principles of our method and the loss function in detail. In Sect. 4, we present the conducted comparative experiments and ablation analysis. Finally, in Sect. 5, we provide the conclusion of this research.

2   Related Work

In this section, we first introduce the traditional and DL-based MEF methods. Next, we briefly introduce the GAN and its variants. Finally, we introduce GhostNet [11] and multiscale networks in brief.

2.1   Existing Multi-exposure Image Fusion Methods

Traditional MEF Methods. Traditional MEF methods utilize manually designed fusion rules to combine images or their features [24]. In a representative approach, the fusion weights are determined by pixel or patch features. [17] designed two functions based on the overall luminance and the global gradient of an image to define the fusion weights. To preserve details and reduce the observed noise, filters such as bilateral filters [44] and median and recursive filters [23] can be applied to define the fusion weights. These methods consider only pixels or their surrounding small areas, often leading to uneven luminance transformations. To address this issue, researchers have defined fusion rules on the basis of patch features. Ma [33] divided an image into nonoverlapping patches and decomposed each patch into three components–signal intensity, signal structure and average intensity components. Then, different fusion rules based on patch intensity and exposure estimates were applied to these components. On this basis, [23,44] improved the effect of fusion in terms of detail preservation and efficiency. However, these methods cannot adapt to diverse scenes [24].

In addition, transform-domain information can also be used to define the fusion rules, and the most representative transform is the multiscale transform.

MEF methods based on the multiscale transform commonly consist of three stages: transforming images into sequences at different resolutions, such as Laplacian pyramids [37, 46], Gaussian pyramids [26], and base and detail layers [25, 55]; manually extracting features and fusing them at each resolution; and reconstructing the images from the sequences. Although these methods fully use multiscale features, handcrafted features extraction and fusion are time-consuming and fail in cases with complex scenes.

DL-Based MEF Methods. Remarkable results in computer vision and image processing have been achieved with DL approaches [21, 27]. Recently, two kinds of DL models have achieved fair performance in MEF tasks: CNNs and GANs [66]. The following briefly introduces the classic MEF algorithms.

For the first time, DeepFuse [43] incorporated DL into the MEF task and employed the MEF structural similarity index measure (MEF-SSIM) [34] as its loss function. On this basis, Qi [40] added the colored MEF-SSIM [31] and an unreferenced gradient fidelity term to the loss function, and the parameters became more comprehensive, achieving better MEF results. Deng [5] simultaneously considered the MEF and superresolution tasks, and proposed a deep coupled feedback network (CF-Net). Han [10] proposed a deep perception enhancement network named DPE-MEF. The abovementioned methods extract image features via convolution operations; thus, they have the inherent limitation of lacking the long-range dependencies between pixels. Qu [41] incorporated a transformer into the MEF framework to address this shortcoming. However, the transformer and CNN modules are two separate submodules in this fusion framework. Ignoring the interactions between local and nonlocal features may result in the loss of details. Im [14] proposed a method to optimize the MEF model by using self-supervised learning to generate reference images and introducing dynamic hyperparameters in the loss function. However, the adjustment of dynamic hyperparameters increases the training complexity and the quality of the reference image directly affects the model results. Additionally, unified learning-based methods are prone to overlooking the differences between image fusion tasks [59, 69], thus resulting in color distortions or exaggerated details.

GANs have also generated significant interest in image processing [47, 50]. Following the first GAN-based MEF model proposed by Xu [60], Yang [64] proposed unsupervised GAN models with two discriminators to distinguish between two source images and their generated counterparts. Le [16] first proposed a generative adversarial network based on continuous learning, which was trained to generate a model with memory, enabling it to memorize what had been learned from previous tasks. This method effectively solves the content forgetting problem during training and has high computational efficiency and a low storage rate. In the above GAN-based MEF methods, the generator uses a convolution operation, so long-range dependencies are still ignored, and the obtained results differ greatly from those of the real sample. Ai [2] proposed a cGAN-based colorization algorithm for infrared images, which improves the generator by adopting a multi-scale feature extraction module, enhancing the capture of features at different scales through three types of convolutions, and introducing an attention mechanism to improve the discriminator's image differentiation ability, reduce color leakage, and improve the semantic clarity of the image. However, in the MEF tasks, relying only on convolution to extract local features is not enough to handle global information, so more complex mechanisms need to be introduced to synthesize global features to ensure that the final fused image has both good details and overall effects.

2.2   GAN and Its Variants

Goodfellow [7] first proposed the concept of a GAN, which includes a generator and a discriminator. The generator tries to generate realistic fake data to fool the discriminator, and the discriminator attempts to distinguish a result produced by the generator from the corresponding GT through simultaneous training. This antagonism is essentially a zero-sum game that tends to lead to shocks and instability during the training process.

To avoid this problem, researchers have improved the architectures or loss functions used to construct networks, such as deep convolutional GANs (DCGANs) [42], least- squares GANs (LSGANs) [36], Wasserstein GANs (WGANs) [3], and conditional GANs (cGANs) [38]. An LSGAN adopts the least-squares loss function to replace the sigmoid cross-entropy loss function. Additionally, its generator cannot generate fake samples when the source samples are very complex because the feedback information given by the discriminator is quite limited. A cGAN combines valid information that is related to the given source samples but different from the information of the generator or the discriminator to drive the network to find the optimal solution in the desired direction.

In our approach, we use a cGAN as the main framework and choose the average of the input images as the valid information for providing more detailed information to the model. Utilizing the least-squares loss function prevents the gradient from disappearing and produces a higher-quality image.

2.3   GhostNet

Han [11] proposed a lightweight network called GhostNet. Researchers have reported that although GhostNet can significantly reduce computational cost, the representation capability of the model is weakened, and the long-range dependencies between spatial pixels are ignored. On this basis, Tang [48] proposed GhostNetV2, which introduces a decoupled fully connected (DFC) attention mechanism for capturing long-range dependencies to enhance the expanded features. Therefore, we integrate GhostNetV2 into our method to simultaneously aggregate short- and long-range information.

2.4   Multiscale Network

A multiscale network was proposed by [45] for semantic segmentation tasks. This network has a multiscale encoder-decoder structure, and skips connections are used to extract local information from images. Recently, various image fusion models have integrated multiscale networks [10,35,57] for extracting local features. Ma [35] achieves multifocal image fusion by employing GAN networks with different depths. Specifically, the method decomposes the image into different scales and then inputs these different scales and features into GAN networks with different depths, thus realizing image fusion at multiple scales. However, during the multi-scale fusion process, the GAN networks of different depths may produce inconsistent features, which may lead to artifacts or other unnatural visual effects in the fused image. Wang and Wu [53] proposed a multi-scale feature aggregation method for image deraining that recovers the affected image by three coding structural blocks with different dilation rates. However, a single-branch multiscale network is limited in terms of feature presentation. In this case, we utilize a multiscale network to augment the feature extraction process, thereby enhancing the performance and robustness of our model.

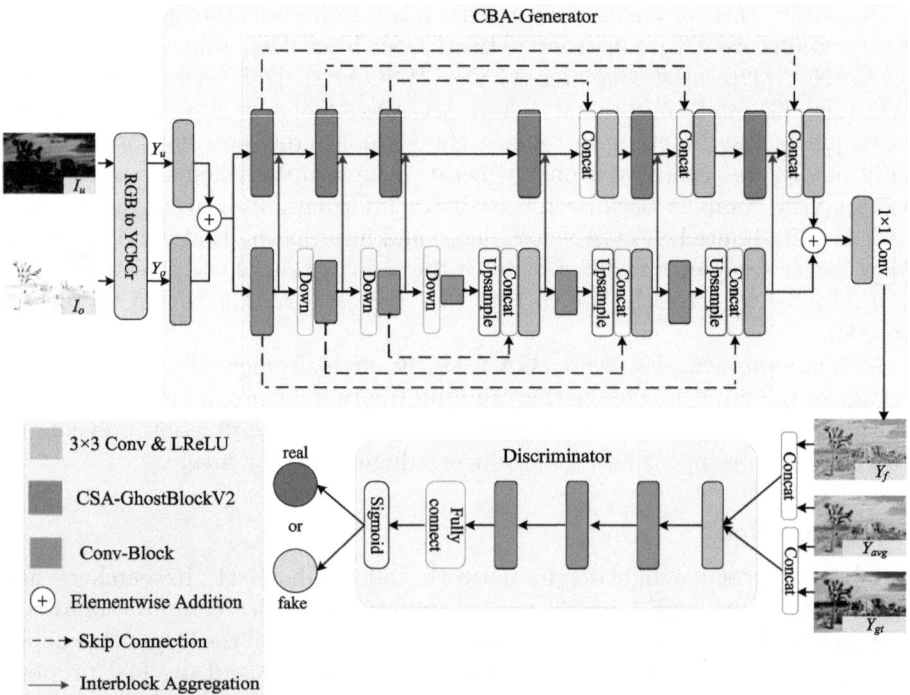

Fig. 2. The overall network architecture of the cross-scale bilevel aggregation-based conditional generative adversarial network (CBA-cGAN). The network comprises a cross-scale bilevel aggregation (CBA) generator and a fully convolutional discriminator. Passing the average image as effective information to the discriminator generates more realistic results.

3   Method

This section describes the overall workflow of our method and the detailed network architecture of the CBA-cGAN.

3.1   Overview

The proposed method takes two RGB images with a large gap between their exposure levels, $I_u \in \mathbb{R}^{H \times W \times 3}$ and $I_o \in \mathbb{R}^{H \times W \times 3}$, as inputs, where H and W represent the height and width of each image, respectively. In the YCbCr color space, the luminance (Y) channel presents brightness and structural details, whereas the chrominance channels Cb and Cr present color information. Thus, similar to some works [18,32,43], two RGB images are transferred to the YCbCr color space. Then, only the Y channel is fed into the CBA-cGAN, and the Cb and Cr channels are fused by weighted summation.

The overall architecture of the proposed CBA-cGAN is shown in Fig. 2. We propose a cross-scale bilevel aggregation (CBA) generator to capture short-range and multiscale long-range dependencies and a conditional discriminator to generate more realistic results; these components are discussed in detail in Sects. 3.2 and 3.4, respectively. The output of the CBA generator is the fused Y channel $Y_f \in \mathbb{R}^{H \times W \times 1}$.

Color information is reliable for the chrominance channels Cb and Cr when the chrominance value is close to 128. Thus, we define the weight of the distance of the chrominance value to 128. Equation (1) represents the fused chrominance channel Cx_f.

$$Cx_f = \frac{Cx_o |Cx_o - \tau| + Cx_u |Cx_u - \tau|}{|Cx_o - \tau| + |Cx_u - \tau|} \tag{1}$$

where Cx_o and Cx_u denote the Cb (or Cr) channels of the overexposed image and underexposed image, respectively, in which parameter τ is set to 128. Finally, the concatenation of Y_f, Cb_f and Cr_f is converted from YCbCr back to the RGB color space to obtain the resulting image.

3.2   Cross-Scale Bilevel Aggregation Generator

The architecture of the CBA generator is shown in Fig. 2. Given the input Y channels of the images $Y_u, Y_o \in \mathbb{R}^{H \times W \times 1}$, a 3×3 convolutional layer and leaky rectified linear unit (LReLU) activation are first applied to extract the shallow features. The initial fused feature F_0 is the sum of the shallow features and is expressed as follows:

$$F_0 = conv_3 (Y_o) + conv_3 (Y_u) \tag{2}$$

where $conv_3(\cdot)$ is a 3×3 convolution layer with LReLU activation. Then, F_0 goes through the two subnetworks of the core part of the generator. One subnetwork is the ULN, which is used to extract multiscale local features, and the other is CSA-GhostNetV2, which aggregates short-range and multiscale long-range dependencies.

The ULN contains the same six convolution blocks, called Conv-Blocks, that extract features at different scales, i.e., $H \times W$, $\frac{H}{2} \times \frac{W}{2}$, $\frac{H}{4} \times \frac{W}{4}$, and $\frac{H}{8} \times \frac{W}{8}$. Each Conv-Block contains two 3×3 convolutional layers for extracting the local features at a specific scale, and each convolutional layer is successively followed by batch normalization (BN) and LReLU activation to avoid exploding gradients, thereby speeding up the convergence process. From the first block to the fourth block, downsampling is applied via maximum pooling between each pair of adjacent blocks, whereas from the fourth block to the last block, bilinear interpolation-based upsampling is applied between each pair of adjacent blocks. Additionally, to prevent information losses, the upsampled outputs of the sixth, fifth, and fourth blocks are concatenated with the outputs of the first, second, and third blocks, respectively. The output of the i-th Conv-Block F_i^U is quantified as follows:

$$F_i^U = Conv - Block_i \left(\varphi \left(F_{i-1}^U, F_{8-i}^U \right) \right) \tag{3}$$

where $\varphi \left(\cdot \right)$ represents the process performed before entering the i-th Conv-Block and is defined as:

$$\varphi \left(F_{i-1}^U, F_{8-i}^U \right) = \begin{cases} F_0 & , i = 1 \\ Down_2 \left(F_{i-1}^U \right) & , i \in \{2, 3, 4\} \\ CC \left(Upsample_2 \left(F_{i-1}^U \right), F_{8-i}^U \right) & , i \in \{5, 6\} \end{cases} \tag{4}$$

where $Down_2(\cdot)$ and $Upsample_2(\cdot)$ are the downsampling and bilinear interpolation-based upsampling operations, respectively, with scales of 2, and $CC(\cdot)$ is a concatenation operation followed by a 3×3 convolutional layer with LReLU activation, which is used to adjust the number of channels. The first and upsampled of the last Conv-Block is subsequently concatenated as the output of the ULN.

CSA-GhostNetV2 contains six identical blocks, which are called cross-scale aggregation GhostBlockV2s (CSA-GhostBlockV2s). CSA-GhostBlockV2 integrates multiscale context features with long-range dependencies. The structure of this type of block is discussed in detail in Sect. 3.3. Additionally, the outputs of the sixth, fifth, and fourth blocks are concatenated with the outputs of the first, second, and third blocks, respectively, to prevent information losses. However, CSA-GhostBlockV2 relies on simple linear transformations to generate features. While this reduces computational complexity, it also limits the network's ability to capture complex local structures in the image, potentially resulting in the under-representation of fine-grained local features. To address this problem, we propose an interblock aggregation process by employing the addition operation on the outputs of the CSA-GhostBlockV2s and Conv-Blocks. Specifically, we implement a bilinear interpolation-based upsampling operation on the Conv-Block to match the spatial resolution of the corresponding CSA-GhostBlockV2. Mathematically, the output of the i-th CSA-GhostBlockV2 F_i^C is calculated as:

$$F_i^C = CSA - GhostBlockV2_i \left(\delta \left(F_{i-1}^C, F_i^U, F_{8-i}^C \right) \right) \tag{5}$$

where $\delta\left(\cdot\right)$ represents the process before entering CSA-GhostBlockV2 and is defined as :

$$\delta\left(F_{i-1}^{C}, F_{i}^{U}, F_{8-i}^{C}\right) =$$

$$\begin{cases} F_0 & ,i=1 \\ F_{i-1}^{C} + Upsample_r\left(F_i^U\right) & ,i \in \{2,3,4\} \\ CC\left(F_{8-i}^{C}, F_{i-1}^{C} + Upsample_r\left(CC\left(F_{8-i}^{U}, Upsample_2\left(F_{i-1}^{U}\right)\right)\right)\right) & ,i \in \{5,6\} \end{cases}$$

$$(6)$$

where $Upsample_r(\cdot)$ is a bilinear interpolation-based upsampling operation with a scale of r, i.e., 2 or 4. The outputs of the ULN and the last CSA-GhostBlockV2 are then concatenated as the output of CSA-GhostNetV2.

Finally, the outputs of CSA-GhostNetV2 and the ULN are added, and this step is followed by two convolutional layers. The first is a 3×3 convolutional layer with LReLU activation, and the other is a 1×1 convolutional layer for transforming the output feature to the fused Y channel Y_f.

3.3   CSA-GhostBlockV2

GhostBlockV2 [48] can combine local and global features but operates at a single scale. As a result, GhostBlockV2 struggles to gather sufficient multiscale context information. We extend GhostBlockV2 with depthwise dilated separable convolutions possessing multiple dilation rates to fully combine the context information with long-range dependencies. We take the i-th CSA-GhostBlockV2 as an example (Fig. 3), which utilizes the aggregation features $\delta\left(F_{i-1}^{C}, F_{i}^{U}, F_{8-i}^{C}\right)$ as its inputs. To simplify the notation, we use F_i^A to represent $\delta\left(F_{i-1}^{C}, F_{i}^{U}, F_{8-i}^{C}\right)$. First, F_i^A passes through two branches: a DFC attention module for capturing long-range dependencies and a cross-scale aggregation ghost (CSA-Ghost) module for extracting multiscale contextual information. Next, the enhanced features obtained by conducting elementwise multiplication on the $DFC(F_i^A)$ and $G^1(F_i^A)$ acquired from these two branches are fed into the second

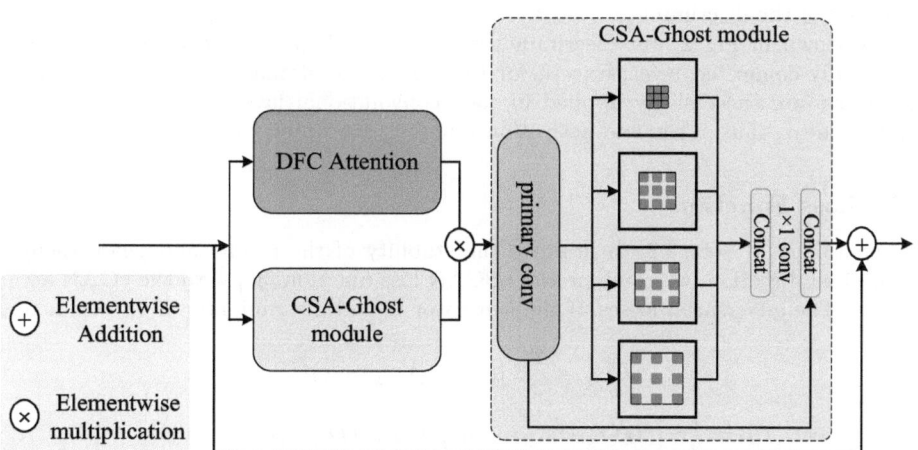

Fig. 3. The architecture of the cross-scale aggregation GhostBlockV2 (CSA-GhostBlockV2).

CSA-Ghost module to obtain large-scale long-range image features. Finally, the input features are summed with the output of the second CSA-Ghost module. Mathematically, this process can be calculated as follows:

$$CSA - GhostBlockV2_i \left(F_i^A \right) = G^2 \left(G^1 \left(F_i^A \right) \odot DFC \left(F_i^A \right) \right) + F_i^A \qquad (7)$$

where $G^1(\cdot)$ and $G^2(\cdot)$ are the first and second CSA-Ghost modules, respectively; $DFC(\cdot)$ denotes the DFC attention operation; and $\odot$ denotes elementwise multiplication.

The CSA-Ghost module contains a primary convolution operation for extracting intrinsic features and a multiscale cheap operation for capturing the contextual features located at different scales. The primary convolution operation consists of a 1×1 pointwise convolution layer with BN and a rectified linear unit (ReLU). The multiscale cheap operation contains four parallel depthwise dilated separable convolution operations with dilation rates of 1, 2, 3, and 4. By incorporating dilated convolutions with varying dilation rates, the intrablock aggregation mechanism is enhanced, and both detailed and global features are effectively captured. This facilitates cross-scale feature extraction and fusion. Then, we use a concatenation operation followed by a 1×1 convolution operation to aggregate the contextual features observed at different scales. Finally, the intrinsic features are concatenated with the aggregated contextual features along the channel dimension to obtain the outputs of the CSA-Ghost module.

3.4   Discriminator

The discriminator plays an adversarial game against the generator to make the generated image similar to the ground truth. The inclusion of conditions is an effective method for addressing the pattern collapse issue encountered in GANs [38]. The average image contains the global visual perception of the source images, which can provide a more accurate reference for the generator and prevent the unbalanced exposure of the generated image, thereby reducing the incoherent or unnatural areas in the image and producing a more natural fusion image. Thus, we use the average image as the condition of the discriminator.

As shown in Fig. 2, our discriminator consists of four 3×3 convolutional layers and a fully connected layer. Except for the first convolutional layer, BN and LReLU operations are successively applied in each convolutional layer. The fully connected layer is linear; thus, a sigmoid activation function is adopted to generate a scalar.

3.5   Loss Function

As mentioned in Sect. 2.2, to improve the stability of the results and guide them in the desired direction, we combine the LSGAN loss function [36] with the cGAN architecture. The adversarial losses of the generator G and discriminator D are defined as follows:

$$\mathcal{L}_{adv} = \frac{1}{2} \mathbb{E} \left[(D\left(Y_f | Y_{avg}\right) - c)^2 \right] \qquad (8)$$

$$\mathcal{L}_D = \frac{1}{2} \mathbb{E} \left[(D\left(Y_{gt} | Y_{avg}\right) - b)^2 \right] + \frac{1}{2} \mathbb{E} \left[(D\left(Y_f | Y_{avg}\right) - a)^2 \right] \qquad (9)$$

where $\mathbb{E}[\cdot]$ indicates the expectation calculation and Y_f, Y_{avg}, and Y_{gt} denote the luma components of the fused image, the average image, and the GT, respectively. a, b, and c are constants that satisfy the conditions $b - c = 1$ and $b - a = 2$ [36].

To further improve the stability of the model and preserve structural features, we introduce the SSIM as a reconstruction loss [13] to measure the perceptual difference between Y_f and Y_{gt}. Equation (10) is the definition of the SSIM loss function.

$$\mathcal{L}_{ssim} = 1 - SSIM\,(Y_f, Y_{gt}) \tag{10}$$

Additionally, to preserve details, the gradient loss is explored and defined as follows:

$$\mathcal{L}_{grad} = \|Grad\,(Y_f) - Grad\,(Y_{gt})\|_2 \tag{11}$$

where $\|\cdot\|_2$ is the ℓ_2-norm and $Grad(\cdot)$ is calculated as follows:

$$Grad\,(Y) = mean\,(|Y_x| + |Y_y|) \tag{12}$$

where Y_x and Y_y are the gradients computed by the horizontal and vertical Sobel operators, respectively. The total loss of generator G is defined as follows:

$$\mathcal{L}_G = \alpha\mathcal{L}_{adv} + \beta\mathcal{L}_{ssim} + \lambda\mathcal{L}_{grad} \tag{13}$$

where the hyperparameters α, β, and λ are set to 10^{-3}, 10^2, and 10^3, respectively.

4   Experimental Results

In this section, we begin by introducing the utilized dataset and detailed experimental configurations. Then, we present a comprehensive analysis by providing both qualitative and quantitative comparison results obtained on two widely used datasets. In addition, we conduct ablation experiments to demonstrate the effectiveness of our CBA-cGAN.

4.1   Configurations

Dataset. The data are acquired from SICE, which is a public MEF dataset [4] that contains 589 multiexposure image sequences with different exposure values, each with a GT. Its image scenes are rich and diverse. A total of 489 SICE image sequences and GTs are selected for training, and the remaining 100 sets are used for testing. Two images in each image sequence with a large gap between their exposure levels are selected as our source inputs to verify the fusion performance of our method. To increase the credibility of our proposed method, we also select 20 image pairs from another public dataset (HRP[1]) [58] as a new test set. The HRP dataset contains 169 image pairs without GT. From this set, we selected 20 image pairs with significant exposure differences for testing.

Implementation Details. Our experiments are deployed on an Nvidia A100 GPU with PyTorch as the base framework. The model parameters are updated and converged via the Adam optimization algorithm [15], and its initial learning rate is set to 0.0001. The batch size is 15. To speed up the training process of the network, we resize the source images to 512×512.

---

[1] https://github.com/hangxiaotian/Perceptual-Multi-exposure-Image-Fusion.

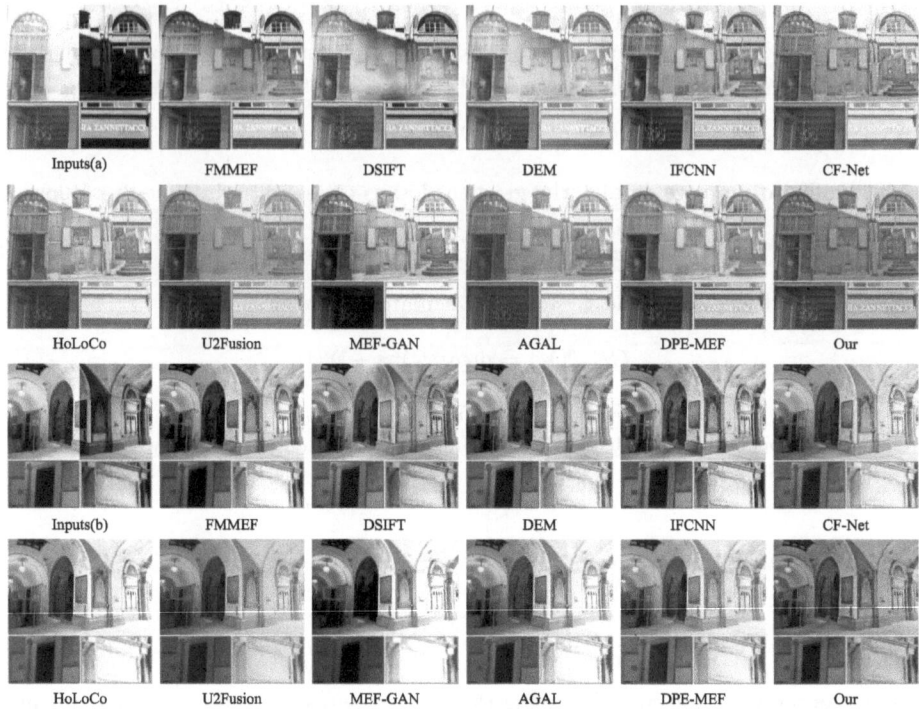

Fig. 4. Comparative visualization of the results obtained on the SICE dataset. Local details are indicated by red and green boxes, respectively. (Color figure online)

Evaluation Metrics. Referring to prior work, we use six important image quality evaluation metrics: feature mutual information (FMI) [9], phase congruency (Q_P) [70], the gradient-based similarity measure ($Q^{AB/F}$) [62], visual information fidelity (VIF) [12], Peilla's metric (Q_W) [39], and the MEF-SSIM [34]. FMI measures the amount of feature information transferred from the source image to the fused image; the higher its value is, the greater the degree of feature transfer. Q_P and $Q^{AB/F}$ measure the image features; higher values represent better fusion performance. The VIF is used to evaluate how strongly the fusion results conforms to human visual perception; the higher the VIF is, the better the visual effect. Q_W and the MEF-SSIM are based on the structures of image similarity metrics; higher values also indicate better image quality. All indicators are calculated via the code provided in [68].

Performance Evaluation. We compare the performance of the proposed methods with that of ten current state-of-the-art methods, including three traditional MEF methods (FMMEF [19], DSIFT [30], and DEM [55]) and seven DL-based MEF methods (MEF-GAN [60], U2Fusion [59], IFCNN [69], AGAL [28], HoLoCo [29], DPE-MEF [10], and CF-Net [5]). Specifically, FMMEF is based on structural patch decomposition. DSIFT obtains fusion results via a scale-invariant feature transformation. The DEM transfers the input images to the YUV color space and obtains fusion results via a multiscale operation. The MEF-GAN fuses exposed images under extreme conditions via the original GAN. U2Fusion and the IFCNN are two unified image fusion models that are also applicable to MEF tasks. AGAL is a GAN-based method with two discriminators. HoLoCo uses contrastive learning for MEF. DPE-MEF is a depth perception enhancement network designed to restore details while preserving the color fidelity of the input image. CF-Net provides a coupled feedback network that performs both MEF and superresolution tasks. We obtain the results for the comparison methods via the official code and optimal network weights provided by the authors.

4.2 Subjective and Objective Comparisons Conducted on the SICE Dataset

Qualitative Comparisons. In this section, we select 4 image pairs from the SICE test set to conduct a visual comparison with ten methods. We comprehensively evaluate these methods from two perspectives: local details and global perception capabilities. Figures 4 and 5 show the results of the comparative visualization. We impose two local boxes on the image, which are presented in red and green, to more concretely evaluate all the methods and demonstrate the superiority of our methods in terms of their visual effects. For local information, we select the clearest portions from the original image to showcase the restoration performance of each method.

The traditional methods reveal many localized dark areas in their FMMEF and DSIFT results. Moreover, the exposure of the DEM results is not balanced, which tends to cause detail losses in overexposed or underexposed areas, such as Inputs(b) in Fig. 4. Compared with the DL-based methods, the IFCNN and U2Fusion, which are multitask image fusion methods, fail to consider multilevel image features. The IFCNN produces a strange color tone, and the result of U2Fusion fades overall. CF-Net provides blurry and flawed results, and HoLoCo yields an unclear visualization. The MEF-GAN does not effectively recover information in extremely dark or bright conditions, and its exposure effect is not uniform. AGAL presents color distortions in its results. The texture of the DPE-MEF results is not sufficiently clear, e.g., in the clouds of Inputs(d) in Fig. 5. The fusion results also appear noisy due to the unsmooth processed details, e.g., the doorframe of Inputs(b) in Fig. 4. Visually, the fusion results obtained via our method effectively preserve the important information of the source image, enhance its details without over-exaggeration, and deliver superior visual effects.

Quantitative Comparisons. We use 100 image pairs acquired from the SICE test dataset and calculate the average scores produced by each of the 10 methods in terms of the six metrics. We describe the employed evaluation metrics in the experimental setup section. Table 1 reports the results of the quantitative analysis.

The data in the table show that the metrics of the traditional methods are largely higher than the metrics of the proposed DL-based methods. As shown in Fig. 4, FMMEF is not visually effective because of the presence of large localized dark areas, but its VIF, a metric based on human visual perception, is the highest. Specifically, under extreme exposure conditions, the traditional methods yield subjective visual effects that are inconsistent with the objective evaluation results. In contrast, the subjective effects of the DL-based methods are generally consistent with the objective evaluations. Therefore, in this case, we analyze the quantitative comparison results generated by the DL-based methods.

As shown in Table 1, among the DL-based methods, the proposed method achieves the best Q_P, $Q^{AB/F}$, Q_W, and MEF-SSIM values on the SICE test set, which indicates that our method has better fusion performance than that of the competing approaches and that its fusion results are more reproducible for real scenes. The FMI obtained

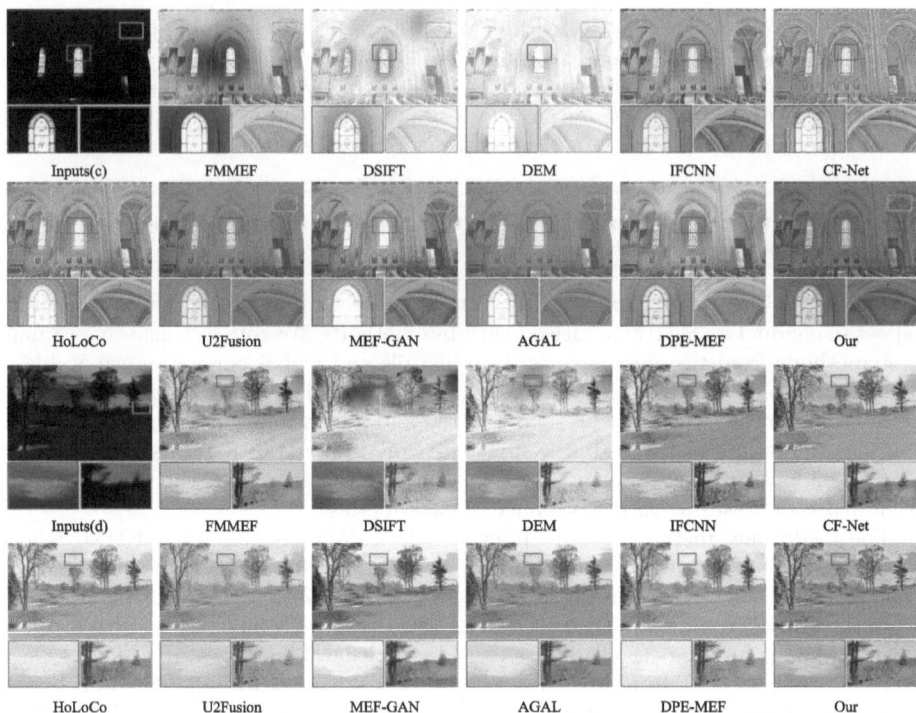

Fig. 5. Comparative visualization of the results obtained on the SICE dataset. Local details are indicated by red and green boxes, respectively. (Color figure online)

Table 1. This table presents the results of a quantitative comparison conducted among the 10 methods on the test data in SICE. We choose six important objective evaluation indicators.

Methods	FMI	Q_P	$Q^{AB/F}$	VIF	Q_W	MEF-SSIM
FMMEF	0.8903	0.6978	0.7594	0.9200	0.8901	0.9871
DSIFT	0.8883	0.6674	0.7242	0.7664	0.8801	0.9546
DEM	0.8919	0.6747	0.7467	0.8444	0.9153	0.9753
IFCNN	0.8591	0.5724	0.5335	1.0843	0.7703	0.9246
CF-Net	0.8409	0.1479	0.3346	0.7264	0.5784	0.8921
HoLoCo	0.8544	0.2743	0.3764	0.7381	0.5499	0.9117
U2Fusion	0.8750	0.5625	0.6245	0.5850	0.8209	0.9418
MEF-GAN	0.8575	0.3224	0.4001	0.7360	0.5781	0.8981
AGAL	0.8659	0.5614	0.6219	0.6986	0.8196	0.9441
DPE-MEF	0.8685	0.5663	0.6201	0.7867	0.8415	0.9485
Ours	0.8730	0.6216	0.6700	0.7562	0.8478	0.9588

Note: Red, Blue represent 1st, 2nd place respectively.

by the CBA-cGAN is the second-best value, indicating that our method can transmit richer detail information to the fused image. The VIF metric is the third-best value,

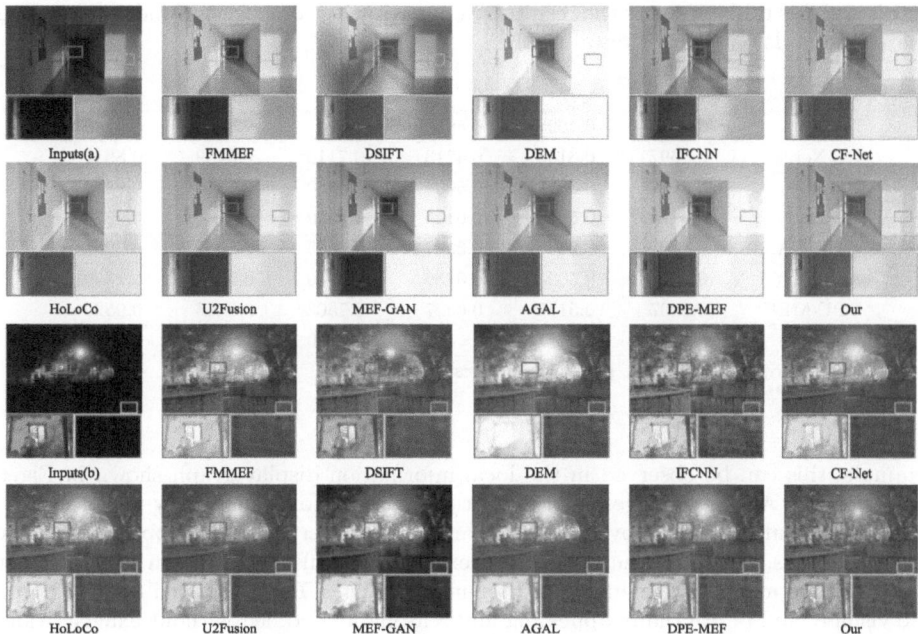

Fig. 6. Comparative visualization of the results obtained on the HRP dataset. Local details are indicated by red and green boxes, respectively. (Color figure online)

indicating that a good visualization is produced for our fusion results. Overall, the method demonstrates superior fusion performance on the SICE dataset, outperforming other methods in both visualization and evaluation metrics.

4.3   Subjective and Objective Comparisons Conducted on the HRP Dataset

Qualitative Comparisons. To increase the credibility of the proposed method and reduce the risk of overfitting, we use the HRP dataset to test our model trained on SICE. A comparative visualization of the tested methods is shown in Fig. 6. The figures show that on other test datasets, our results still maintain good visualization effects and maximize the preservation of the detailed information contained in the source images. However, obvious localized black patches appear in the results of the traditional methods such as DSIFT. The exposure effect of the DEM is unbalanced, and details are badly lost. FMMEF has no visible artifacts but suffers from overexposure. Among those of the DL approaches, the fused images obtained by U2Fusion and the MEF-GAN have poor colors and do not recover to the normal exposure level. U2Fusion has raw perception, and the MEF-GAN suffers from localized areas with grayish darkness. The fusion results obtained by the IFCNN on HRP are slightly better than those obtained on SICE, but an observation of the localized portion of its fused image shows that the details are too exaggerated. When combined with the superresolution task, CF-Net maintains the overall color fidelity of the input image but falls short in terms of handling fine details, resulting in reduced clarity in certain areas. For

Table 2. This table presents the results of a quantitative comparison conducted among the 10 methods on the test data in HRP.

Methods	FMI	Q_P	$Q^{AB/F}$	VIF	Q_W	MEF-SSIM
IFCNN	0.8849	0.4998	0.5959	0.9330	0.8253	0.9338
CF-Net	0.8697	0.3153	0.4713	0.7113	0.6489	0.8941
HoLoCo	0.8839	0.3831	0.5008	0.6830	0.6545	0.9229
U2Fusion	0.8975	0.5044	0.6169	0.5592	0.8143	0.9377
MEF-GAN	0.8801	0.2660	0.3937	0.6665	0.5469	0.8967
AGAL	0.8933	0.5023	0.6136	0.5950	0.7994	0.9350
DPE-MEF	0.8907	0.5157	0.6427	0.7503	0.8466	0.9520
Ours	0.8982	0.5417	0.6595	0.7139	0.8515	0.9530

Note: Red, Blue represent 1st, 2nd place respectively.

example, this can be observed in the local information display graph shown in Fig. 6 for Inputs(b). AGAL produces color distortions, and HoLoCo has blurry fusion results. The fused results obtained by DPE-MEF are much better than those obtained by the other methods. However, the problem of excessive details remains. On different test datasets, our model still exhibits good generalizability. The generated fusion results are visually and perceptually appealing and reasonably detailed without exaggeration.

Quantitative Comparisons. According to the discussion presented in Sect. 4.2, we do not include traditional methods in the quantitative comparisons. The HRP test dataset in Sect. 4.1 is used for testing our proposed method with seven other DL-based methods to obtain corresponding fused images. To better demonstrate the performance of our method, we first conduct an overall comparison in Table 2 and then provide a more detailed comparison of the metrics produced for each pair of images in Fig. 7. According to the data presented in Table 2, our method achieves the best values for five metrics and the second-best value for the remaining metric. This finding indicates that our method still exhibits excellent fusion performance on different datasets. As seen from the image-by-image metric comparison in Fig. 7, our method produces stable and satisfactory results for different images, further demonstrating its superiority and applicability. Overall, the fusion performance of this method on the HRP dataset remains outstanding compared to other methods.

4.4 Ablation Analysis

To prove the effectiveness of our model, we conduct research on five variants of the proposed model. We use only single-branch CSA-GhostNetV2 to extract the global and local features uniformly in the first variant (SV). SV is used to prove that a double-branch network is more capable of global context information than a single-branch CSA-GhostNetV2. All four of the following variants retain the two-branch network architecture. The second variant (DV1) replaces the first CSA-Ghost module in CSA-GhostBlockV2 with the original ghost module and leaves everything else unchanged. The third variant (DV2) replaces the second CSA-Ghost module in CSA-GhostBlockV2 with the original ghost module and leaves everything else unchanged. The fourth variant (DV3) replaces both the CSA-Ghost module in CSA-GhostBlockV2 with the original

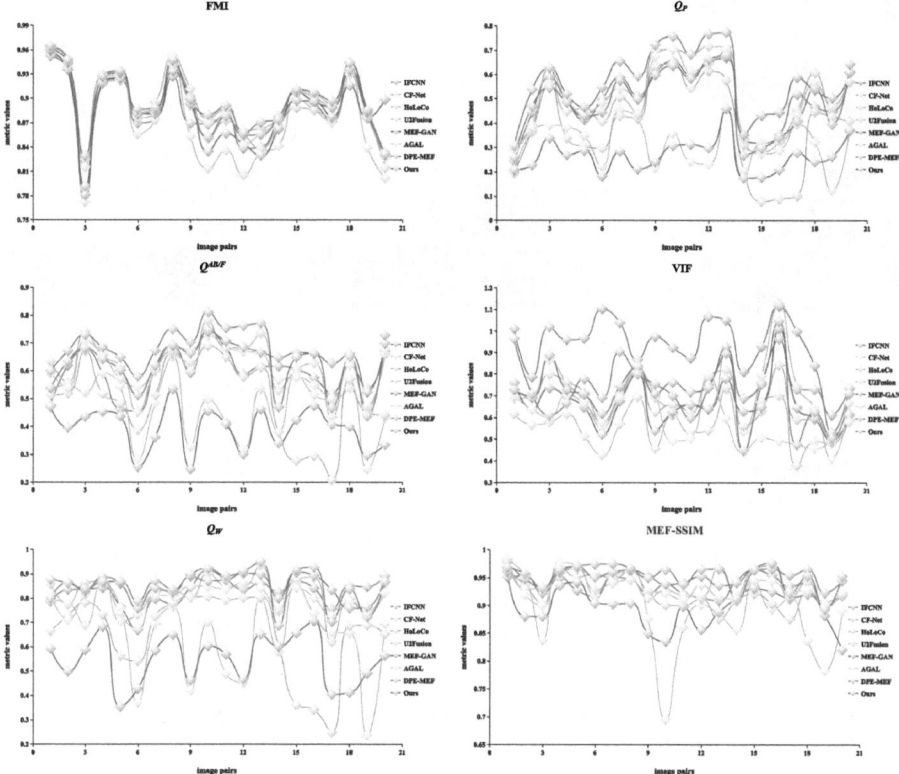

Fig. 7. Detailed metric comparison of 20 image pairs in the HRP. The horizontal axis represents image pairs and the vertical axis represents indicator values. Different line colors represent different methods.

ghost module; otherwise, everything else remains unchanged. The fifth variant (DV4) removes the DFC attention; otherwise, everything else remains unchanged. As shown in the first row of Table 3, the values of the six indicators produced by the single subnetwork are smaller than those of the dual subnetworks. As shown in Fig. 8, the local features derived from the ULN have an important effect on the MEF task, and the dual subnetworks can effectively produce rich local and global context features to achieve improved image quality.

We compare DV1 through DV4, as shown in rows 2 to 5 of Table 3. The intrablock cross-scale aggregation process can add rich contextual features to the network. In addition, DFC attention validates its importance in terms of capturing long-range dependencies. As demonstrated in Fig. 9, our method achieves satisfactory performance in terms of both color and detail. Even in night-time environments, it can still recover visible content, further validating the effectiveness of the modules contained in our method.

Inputs   SV   Our

Fig. 8. Visual comparative analysis between SV and our method on the SICE dataset. Local details are indicated by blue and yellow boxes, respectively. (Color figure online)

Table 3. Quantitative comparison among the results of ablation studies conducted on 100 test image sequences in SICE.

Methods	FMI	Q_P	$Q^{AB/F}$	VIF	Q_W	MEF-SSIM
SV	0.8709	0.5974	0.6527	0.6716	0.8264	0.9495
DV1	0.8720	0.6142	0.6610	0.7484	0.8397	0.9581
DV2	0.8718	0.6130	0.6590	0.7502	0.8390	0.9584
DV3	0.8708	0.5975	0.6475	0.7028	0.8280	0.9493
DV4	0.8732	0.6173	0.6673	0.7273	0.8434	0.9561
Ours	0.8730	0.6216	0.6700	0.7562	0.8478	0.9588

Note: Red, Blue represent 1st, 2nd place respectively.

5   Conclusions

In this work, we propose a cross-scale bilevel aggregation-based conditional generative adversarial network. The core part of the generator contains two subnetworks: CSA-GhostNetV2 and a ULN. We extend the original GhostBlockV2 with dilated separable convolutions possessing different dilation rates to aggregate multiscale context information and long-range relationship. An interblock aggregation process integrates the local features extracted by the ULN with the features obtained from CSA-GhostBlockV2 to balance local and global contextual information during the fusion process. A fully convolutional discriminator is used to distinguish the fused image from the corresponding GT. Taking the average image as the condition constrains the global perception of the fused results. Many comparison and ablation implementations show that cross-scale bilevel aggregation can capture notably richer features than those of other methods for improving the obtained fusion result without implementing external postprocessing. At present, the CBA-cGAN operates as a supervised approach, requiring training with GT constraints. However, since the GT selection process is subjective [4], instances in which information may be incomplete are present, potentially resulting in the loss of information in the fusion results. Therefore, exploring extensions of this method to address image fusion challenges in a self-supervised or unsupervised manner represents an important direction for future research.

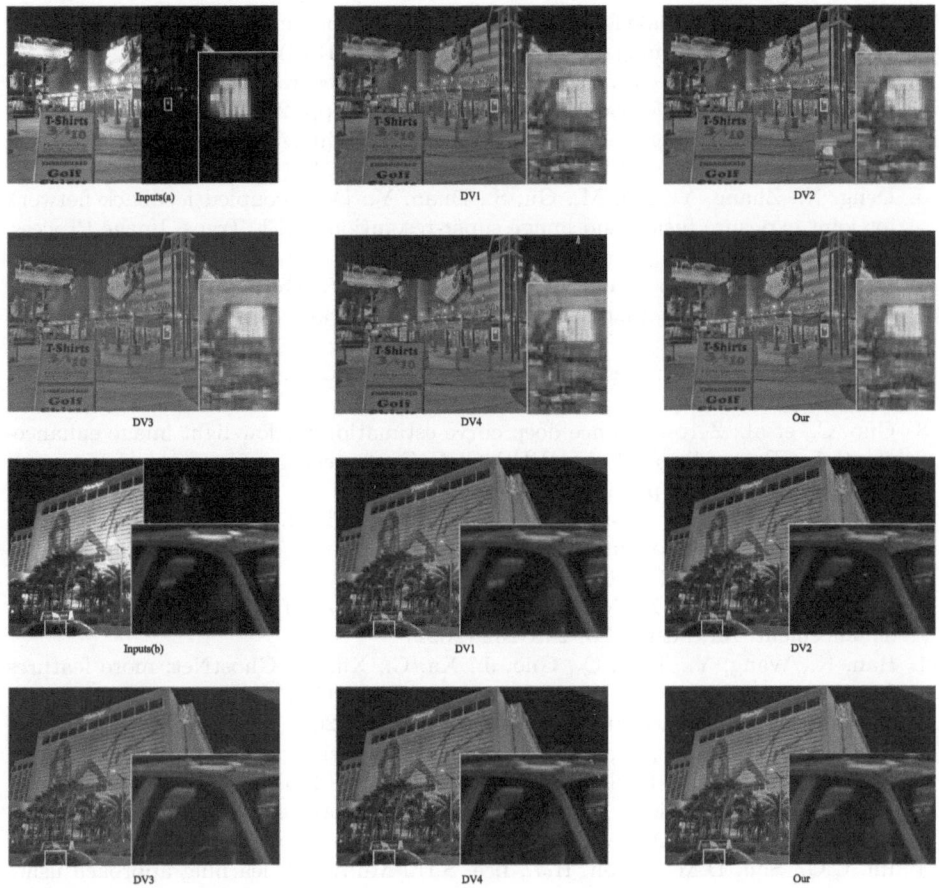

Fig. 9. Visual comparative analysis between DV1 to DV4 and our method on the SICE dataset.

Acknowledgments. This research has been supported in part by the National Natural Science Foundation of China under Grant No. 62066021 and 62206117, and by the Natural Science Foundation of Jiangxi Province under Grant 20232BAB202053 and Grant 20232BAB202054.

Disclosure of Interests. The authors have no competing interests to declare that are relevant to the content of this article.

References

1. Aggarwal, M., Ahuja, N.: Split aperture imaging for high dynamic range. Int. J. Comput. Vision **58**, 7–17 (2004)

2. Ai, Y., et al.: Multi-scale feature fusion with attention mechanism based on CGAN network for infrared image colorization. Appl. Sci. **13**(8), 4686 (2023)

3. Arjovsky, M., Chintala, S., Bottou, L.: Wasserstein generative adversarial networks. In: International Conference on Machine Learning, pp. 214–223. PMLR (2017)

4. Cai, J., Gu, S., Zhang, L.: Learning a deep single image contrast enhancer from multi-exposure images. IEEE Trans. Image Process. **27**(4), 2049–2062 (2018)

5. Deng, X., Zhang, Y., Xu, M., Gu, S., Duan, Y.: Deep coupled feedback network for joint exposure fusion and image super-resolution. IEEE Trans. Image Process. **30**, 3098–3112 (2021)

6. Gharbi, M., Chen, J., Barron, J.T., Hasinoff, S.W., Durand, F.: Deep bilateral learning for real-time image enhancement. ACM Trans. Graph. (TOG) **36**(4), 1–12 (2017)

7. Goodfellow, I., et al.: Generative adversarial networks. Commun. ACM **63**(11), 139–144 (2020)

8. Guo, C., et al.: Zero-reference deep curve estimation for low-light image enhancement. In: Proceedings of the IEEE/CVF Conference on Computer Vision and Pattern Recognition, pp. 1780–1789 (2020)

9. Haghighat, M.B.A., Aghagolzadeh, A., Seyedarabi, H.: A non-reference image fusion metric based on mutual information of image features. Comput. Electr. Eng. **37**(5), 744–756 (2011)

10. Han, D., Li, L., Guo, X., Ma, J.: Multi-exposure image fusion via deep perceptual enhancement. Inf. Fusion **79**, 248–262 (2022)

11. Han, K., Wang, Y., Tian, Q., Guo, J., Xu, C., Xu, C.: GhostNet: more features from cheap operations. In: Proceedings of the IEEE/CVF Conference on Computer Vision and Pattern Recognition, pp. 1580–1589 (2020)

12. Han, Y., Cai, Y., Cao, Y., Xu, X.: A new image fusion performance metric based on visual information fidelity. Inf. fusion **14**(2), 127–135 (2013)

13. Hassan, M., Bhagvati, C.: Structural similarity measure for color images. Int. J. Comput. Appl. **43**(14), 7–12 (2012)

14. Im, C.G., Son, D.M., Kwon, H.J., Lee, S.H.: Multi-task learning approach using dynamic hyperparameter for multi-exposure fusion. Mathematics **11**(7), 1620 (2023)

15. Kingma, D.P., Ba, J.: Adam: a method for stochastic optimization. arXiv preprint arXiv:1412.6980 (2014)

16. Le, Z., et al.: UIFGAN: an unsupervised continual-learning generative adversarial network for unified image fusion. Inf. Fusion **88**, 305–318 (2022)

17. Lee, S.H., Park, J.S., Cho, N.I.: A multi-exposure image fusion based on the adaptive weights reflecting the relative pixel intensity and global gradient. In: 2018 25th IEEE International Conference on Image Processing (ICIP), pp. 1737–1741. IEEE (2018)

18. Lei, J., Li, J., Liu, J., Zhou, S., Zhang, Q., Kasabov, N.K.: GALFusion: multi-exposure image fusion via a global-local aggregation learning network. IEEE Trans. Instrum. Meas. **72**, 1–15 (2023)

19. Li, H., Ma, K., Yong, H., Zhang, L.: Fast multi-scale structural patch decomposition for multi-exposure image fusion. IEEE Trans. Image Process. **29**, 5805–5816 (2020)

20. Li, J., Liu, J., Zhou, S., Zhang, Q., Kasabov, N.K.: Learning a coordinated network for detail-refinement multiexposure image fusion. IEEE Trans. Circuits Syst. Video Technol. **33**(2), 713–727 (2022)

21. Li, L., Liang, D., Gao, Y., Huang, S.J., Chen, S.: ALL-E: aesthetics-guided low-light image enhancement. arXiv preprint arXiv:2304.14610 (2023)

22. Li, M., Liu, J., Yang, W., Sun, X., Guo, Z.: Structure-revealing low-light image enhancement via robust retinex model. IEEE Trans. Image Process. **27**(6), 2828–2841 (2018)
23. Li, S., Kang, X.: Fast multi-exposure image fusion with median filter and recursive filter. IEEE Trans. Consum. Electron. **58**(2), 626–632 (2012)
24. Li, S., Kang, X., Fang, L., Hu, J., Yin, H.: Pixel-level image fusion: a survey of the state of the art. Inf. Fusion **33**, 100–112 (2017)
25. Li, S., Kang, X., Hu, J.: Image fusion with guided filtering. IEEE Trans. Image Process. **22**(7), 2864–2875 (2013)
26. Li, Z., Wei, Z., Wen, C., Zheng, J.: Detail-enhanced multi-scale exposure fusion. IEEE Trans. Image Process. **26**(3), 1243–1252 (2017)
27. Liu, G., Liu, Y., Tang, L., Bavirisetti, D.P., Wang, X.: A generative adversarial network for infrared and visible image fusion using adaptive dense generator and Markovian discriminator. Optik **288**, 171139 (2023)
28. Liu, J., Shang, J., Liu, R., Fan, X.: Attention-guided global-local adversarial learning for detail-preserving multi-exposure image fusion. IEEE Trans. Circuits Syst. Video Technol. **32**(8), 5026–5040 (2022)
29. Liu, J., Wu, G., Luan, J., Jiang, Z., Liu, R., Fan, X.: HoLoCo: holistic and local contrastive learning network for multi-exposure image fusion. Inf. Fusion **95**, 237–249 (2023)
30. Liu, Y., Wang, Z.: Dense sift for ghost-free multi-exposure fusion. J. Vis. Commun. Image Represent. **31**, 208–224 (2015)
31. Ma, K., Duanmu, Z., Yeganeh, H., Wang, Z.: Multi-exposure image fusion by optimizing a structural similarity index. IEEE Trans. Comput. Imaging **4**(1), 60–72 (2017)
32. Ma, K., Duanmu, Z., Zhu, H., Fang, Y., Wang, Z.: Deep guided learning for fast multi-exposure image fusion. IEEE Trans. Image Process. **29**, 2808–2819 (2019)
33. Ma, K., Wang, Z.: Multi-exposure image fusion: a patch-wise approach. In: 2015 IEEE International Conference on Image Processing (ICIP), pp. 1717–1721. IEEE (2015)
34. Ma, K., Zeng, K., Wang, Z.: Perceptual quality assessment for multi-exposure image fusion. IEEE Trans. Image Process. **24**(11), 3345–3356 (2015)
35. Ma, X., Wang, Z., Hu, S., Kan, S.: Multi-focus image fusion based on multi-scale generative adversarial network. Entropy **24**(5), 582 (2022)
36. Mao, X., Li, Q., Xie, H., Lau, R.Y., Wang, Z., Paul Smolley, S.: Least squares generative adversarial networks. In: Proceedings of the IEEE International Conference on Computer Vision, pp. 2794–2802 (2017)
37. Mertens, T., Kautz, J., Van Reeth, F.: Exposure fusion. In: 15th Pacific Conference on Computer Graphics and Applications (PG 2007), pp. 382–390. IEEE (2007)
38. Mirza, M., Osindero, S.: Conditional generative adversarial nets. arXiv preprint arXiv:1411.1784 (2014)
39. Piella, G., Heijmans, H.: A new quality metric for image fusion. In: Proceedings 2003 International Conference on Image Processing (Cat. No. 03CH37429), vol. 3, pp. III–173. IEEE (2003)
40. Qi, Y., et al.: Deep unsupervised learning based on color un-referenced loss functions for multi-exposure image fusion. Inf. Fusion **66**, 18–39 (2021)
41. Qu, L., Liu, S., Wang, M., Song, Z.: TransMEF: a transformer-based multi-exposure image fusion framework using self-supervised multi-task learning. In: Proceedings of the AAAI Conference on Artificial Intelligence, vol. 36, pp. 2126–2134 (2022)

42. Radford, A., Metz, L., Chintala, S.: Unsupervised representation learning with deep convolutional generative adversarial networks. arxiv 2015. arXiv preprint arXiv:1511.06434 (2015)
43. Ram Prabhakar, K., Sai Srikar, V., Venkatesh Babu, R.: DeepFuse: a deep unsupervised approach for exposure fusion with extreme exposure image pairs. In: Proceedings of the IEEE International Conference on Computer Vision, pp. 4714–4722 (2017)
44. Raman, S., Chaudhuri, S.: Bilateral filter based compositing for variable exposure photography. In: Eurographics (Short Papers), pp. 1–4 (2009)
45. Ronneberger, O., Fischer, P., Brox, T.: U-Net: convolutional networks for biomedical image segmentation. In: Navab, N., Hornegger, J., Wells, W., Frangi, A. (eds.) Medical Image Computing and Computer-Assisted Intervention–MICCAI 2015: 18th International Conference, Munich, Germany, 5–9 October 2015, Proceedings, Part III 18, pp. 234–241. Springer, Cham (2015). https://doi.org/10.1007/978-3-319-24574-4_28
46. Shen, J., Zhao, Y., Yan, S., Li, X., et al.: Exposure fusion using boosting Laplacian pyramid. IEEE Trans. Cybern. **44**(9), 1579–1590 (2014)
47. Tan, Z., Gao, M., Li, X., Jiang, L.: A flexible reference-insensitive spatiotemporal fusion model for remote sensing images using conditional generative adversarial network. IEEE Trans. Geosci. Remote Sens. **60**, 1–13 (2021)
48. Tang, Y., Han, K., Guo, J., Xu, C., Xu, C., Wang, Y.: GhostNetV2: enhance cheap operation with long-range attention. Adv. Neural. Inf. Process. Syst. **35**, 9969–9982 (2022)
49. Tumblin, J., Agrawal, A., Raskar, R.: Why i want a gradient camera. In: 2005 IEEE Computer Society Conference on Computer Vision and Pattern Recognition (CVPR 2005), vol. 1, pp. 103–110. IEEE (2005)
50. Umer, R.M., Foresti, G.L., Micheloni, C.: Deep generative adversarial residual convolutional networks for real-world super-resolution. In: Proceedings of the IEEE/CVF Conference on Computer Vision and Pattern Recognition Workshops, pp. 438–439 (2020)
51. Wang, C., He, C., Xu, M.: Fast exposure fusion of detail enhancement for brightest and darkest regions. Vis. Comput. **37**(5), 1233–1243 (2021). https://doi.org/10.1007/s00371-021-02079-5
52. Wang, J., Wang, W., Xu, G., Liu, H.: End-to-end exposure fusion using convolutional neural network. IEICE Trans. Inf. Syst. **101**(2), 560–563 (2018)
53. Wang, J.G., Wu, C.S.: Multi-scale aggregation residual channel attention fusion network for single image deraining. Appl. Sci. **13**(4), 2709 (2023)
54. Wang, L., Yoon, K.J.: Deep learning for HDR imaging: state-of-the-art and future trends. IEEE Trans. Pattern Anal. Mach. Intell. **44**(12), 8874–8895 (2021)
55. Wang, Q., Chen, W., Wu, X., Li, Z.: Detail-enhanced multi-scale exposure fusion in YUV color space. IEEE Trans. Circuits Syst. Video Technol. **30**(8), 2418–2429 (2019)
56. Wu, W., Weng, J., Zhang, P., Wang, X., Yang, W., Jiang, J.: URetinex-Net: retinex-based deep unfolding network for low-light image enhancement. In: Proceedings of the IEEE/CVF Conference on Computer Vision and Pattern Recognition, pp. 5901–5910 (2022)
57. Wu, X., Huang, T.Z., Deng, L.J., Zhang, T.J.: Dynamic cross feature fusion for remote sensing pansharpening. In: Proceedings of the IEEE/CVF International Conference on Computer Vision, pp. 14687–14696 (2021)
58. Xu, F., Liu, J., Song, Y., Sun, H., Wang, X.: Multi-exposure image fusion techniques: a comprehensive review. Remote Sens. **14**(3), 771 (2022)

59. Xu, H., Ma, J., Jiang, J., Guo, X., Ling, H.: U2Fusion: a unified unsupervised image fusion network. IEEE Trans. Pattern Anal. Mach. Intell. **44**(1), 502–518 (2020)
60. Xu, H., Ma, J., Zhang, X.P.: MEF-GAN: multi-exposure image fusion via generative adversarial networks. IEEE Trans. Image Process. **29**, 7203–7216 (2020)
61. Xu, Y., Sun, B.: Color-compensated multi-scale exposure fusion based on physical features. Optik **223**, 165494 (2020)
62. Xydeas, C.S., Petrovic, V., et al.: Objective image fusion performance measure. Electron. Lett. **36**(4), 308–309 (2000)
63. Yang, Y., Zhang, D., Wan, W., Huang, S.: Multi-scale exposure fusion based on multi-visual feature measurement and detail enhancement representation. IEEE Trans. Instrum. Meas. **71**, 1–14 (2022)
64. Yang, Z., Chen, Y., Le, Z., Ma, Y.: GANFuse: a novel multi-exposure image fusion method based on generative adversarial networks. Neural Comput. Appl. **33**, 6133–6145 (2021)
65. Yin, J.L., Chen, B.H., Peng, Y.T.: Two exposure fusion using prior-aware generative adversarial network. IEEE Trans. Multimedia **24**, 2841–2851 (2021)
66. Zhang, H., Xu, H., Tian, X., Jiang, J., Ma, J.: Image fusion meets deep learning: a survey and perspective. Inf. Fusion **76**, 323–336 (2021)
67. Zhang, J., Luo, Y., Huang, J., Liu, Y., Ma, J.: Multi-exposure image fusion via perception enhanced structural patch decomposition. Inf. Fusion **99**, 101895 (2023)
68. Zhang, X.: Benchmarking and comparing multi-exposure image fusion algorithms. Inf. Fusion **74**, 111–131 (2021)
69. Zhang, Y., Liu, Y., Sun, P., Yan, H., Zhao, X., Zhang, L.: IFCNN: a general image fusion framework based on convolutional neural network. Inf. Fusion **54**, 99–118 (2020)
70. Zhao, J., Laganiere, R., Liu, Z.: Performance assessment of combinative pixel-level image fusion based on an absolute feature measurement. Int. J. Innov. Comput. Inf. Control **3**(6), 1433–1447 (2007)

Author Index

S. Zhang and L.-J. Zhang (Eds.): SCF 2024 - ICIOT 2024, LNCS 15427, pp. 133–134, 2025.
https://doi.org/10.1007/978-3-031-77003-6